"It's rare to find a Christian honest. *God Loves Sex* is all ⌐ ... ...ore. I'm grateful the authors tell the truth about a subject so complex and beautiful and ultimately give us hope and guidance to redeem the power of intimacy in our own lives."

—**Donald Miller**, bestselling author of *Blue Like Jazz*
and *A Million Miles in a Thousand Years*

"Wise. Playful. Sacred. Surprising. This is not your average Christian book on sex. This is something better—and it is going to bring clarity, healing, and hope to a *lot* of people. I loved it from the first chapter."

—**John Eldredge**, author of *Wild at Heart*

"I have always loved the Song of Songs, but this book gives me a rich picture of how it can help us to something deeper in our marriage. A really good book. So healing!"

—**Stasi Eldredge**, author of *Captivating* and *Becoming Myself*

"In a world that has gone sexually insane, where sex most often lives in confusion, perversion, compulsion, guilt, and shame, it is wonderful that Allender and Longman use the Bible's sex song to restore sex to its original created beauty. Along the way, with refreshing and liberating honesty, they break the church's code of sexual silence and offer us sex wisdom that only comes when we stop being afraid and start listening to the God who fashioned sex for his glory and our good and who meets us in our sexual struggles with remarkable grace."

Paul David Tripp, author of *Sex & Money: Pleasures
That Leave You Empty and Grace That Satisfies*

"*God Loves Sex* is a rare gift from a masterful joining of an adept Bible scholar and a prominent Christian therapist, author, and professor. With the use of both commentary and fiction, Longman and Allender invite us into the ancient, erotic love poems found in Song of Songs. The Song invites us to desire, enjoy, risk, struggle . . . and to consider 'how our sexuality—holy and broken, beautiful and bent—is used by God to draw us deeper into his love.' This book literally took my breath away."

—**Rose Madrid Swetman**, lead pastor, Vineyard Community Church,
and regional leader, Vineyard Northwest

"It's precisely because God loves sex that the Enemy hates it—turns it into a Mirkwood of entangled abuses and heartbreaks and compulsions, a dark place better skirted than braved. Enter Dan and Tremper, old comrades tenderly fearless enough to open sexuality to a little light and air, to name our shames in a way that relieves us of them and woos us to godly desire and play. Their machetes—the Bible at its most scandalously sexual, and professional psychology (fictionalized in Malcolm!) at its most scandalously Christian. There is probably no one who cannot find herself or himself in this book and therein find new hope."

—**Esther L. Meek**, professor of philosophy, Geneva College

GOD
LOVES
SEX

GOD LOVES SEX

AN HONEST CONVERSATION ABOUT SEXUAL DESIRE AND HOLINESS

DAN B. ALLENDER AND TREMPER LONGMAN III

BakerBooks

a division of Baker Publishing Group

www.BakerBooks.com

© 2014 by Dan B. Allender and Tremper Longman III

Published by Baker Books
a division of Baker Publishing Group
P.O. Box 6287, Grand Rapids, MI 49516-6287
www.bakerbooks.com

Printed in the United States of America

Library of Congress Cataloging-in-Publication Data
Allender, Dan B.
 God loves sex : an honest conversation about sexual desire and holiness / Dan B. Allender and Tremper Longman III.
    pages cm
 Includes bibliographical references and index.
 ISBN 978-0-8010-1566-3 (pbk. : alk. paper)
 1. Sex—Religious aspects—Christianity. I. Title.
BT708.A445 2014
241′.66—dc23   2014018020

Unless otherwise noted, quotations of the Song of Songs come from Tremper Longman III, *The Song of Songs*, New International Commentary on the Old Testament (Grand Rapids: Eerdmans, 2001). Used by permission. The translation has occasionally been altered.

Scripture quotations labeled NIV are from the Holy Bible, New International Version®. NIV®. Copyright © 1973, 1978, 1984, 2011 by Biblica, Inc.™ Used by permission of Zondervan. All rights reserved worldwide. www.zondervan.com

Scripture quotations labeled NRSV are from the New Revised Standard Version of the Bible, copyright © 1989, by the Division of Christian Education of the National Council of the Churches of Christ in the United States of America. Used by permission. All rights reserved.

The Authors are represented by Yates & Yates, www.yates2.com.

14 15 16 17 18 19 20   7 6 5 4 3 2 1

To Alice and Becky
You are the love of our lives

———◦∞∞∞◦———

How beautiful your love, my sister, my bride!
How much better your love than wine
and the scent of your oils than spices!

Song of Songs 4:10

Contents

Contents

Acknowledgments

Adam and his wife were both naked, and they felt no shame.

Genesis 2:25 NIV

God created us as sexual beings. Sexuality is an integral part of the human experience. This statement is true of young and old, male and female—in short, of everyone who breathes.

It is the thesis of this book not only that we should acknowledge this truth but that, as Christians, we should talk honestly about it. While this is not the first or only Christian book to address the issue of sexuality, it is certainly more the exception than the rule. Though few Christian leaders adopt the view, believed and practiced in the Middle Ages, that even marital sex was toxic to spirituality (a view described more fully in the first chapter), sexuality is still a taboo topic in many churches today, and when it is discussed, the focus is typically on what Christians shouldn't say or do in the realm of sexuality.

We need an honest conversation about sex in the context of our Christian pursuit of holiness, and it is our belief that a holy approach to sex is not exclusively focused on the "do nots" of sexuality. Our hope as authors is that this book will invite and encourage discussions among Christians, including sermons, Bible studies, and especially conversations between spouses and among friends of both genders.

You see, we believe that we should not be ashamed of our sexuality. After all, as our title declares, God loves sex.

We want to thank the people who have made this book possible by providing expertise and resources in order that we might write the best book we are capable of writing.

We start by mentioning our gratitude for two anonymous donors who provided significant funds so that we could meet face-to-face at crucial points in the writing of the book over the past couple of years. Through their generosity we were also able to hire an expert stylist, Dan Taylor, who was a tremendous help to us in expressing our thoughts. We also want to thank our researcher, Susan Kim (MA, LMHC, in private practice and on the staff of the Allender Center in Seattle), who brought to our attention the most recent thinking about sexuality.

We have deeply appreciated our relationship with Baker Books and in particular the editors who have improved the book by their queries and suggestions in terms of both content and style. Thank you, Jon Wilcox, Chad Allen, Rebecca Cooper, and James Korsmo.

Our agent, Sealy Yates, not only advised us well as we chose a publisher but was also the one who suggested the title of the book.

Finally, and most importantly, we want to express our love and thanks to Becky, Dan's wife, and Alice, Tremper's wife. Not only are they inspiration in terms of the topic of this book, but they have also read it and given us extremely helpful feedback.

Introduction

Holy Sex

God loves sex. He conceived, created, and blessed the process by which our bodies know and are known through desire, arousal, foreplay, intercourse, orgasm, and rest.

Sex is meant by God to be one of the bridge experiences between earth and heaven. It awakens and intersects our deepest physical and spiritual desires. Sex, like music, fills us simultaneously with notes of an intense immanent bodily pleasure and with the sonorous reverberations of another world that is transcendent and holy.

It is no wonder that the enemy of God is relentlessly committed to fouling both immanent pleasure and transcendent joy. Evil hates sex and is ruthlessly committed to tearing down the bridge between desire and holiness.

Real People, Real Struggles

Real people have real sexual struggles. Here is a glimpse of folks sitting near you on a Sunday morning.

Kevin

Kevin is an elder in his church, married, with three children between eight and fourteen years old. He is a kind, generous man whom everyone in his community turns to for emotional support and wisdom. His wife recently discovered a file on his computer with emails from another elder's wife that indicate a growing, intense relationship that has crossed a line into the beginnings of an emotional affair. Her emails often detail how she feels in his presence and how she wishes they were married. He attempts to encourage her by telling her how beautiful she looked at church.

Helene

Helene is twenty-four and a student in a seminary where she is being trained to be a pastor. She is a virgin, wore a purity ring given to her by her father, and has waited to kiss her fiancé until at the altar on their wedding day. She feels like a fake because she often struggles in dreams with images of unclothed women being fondled by other women. She doesn't think she is gay, but she will masturbate to those images a few times a month. Her parents were so strict about sex that they asked her to cover her eyes if a television show portrayed two unmarried people kissing. But when they visited her grandparents, her parents said nothing about the pornography that was stacked in a magazine rack next to the only commode in the house.

Matthew

Matthew is newly divorced and just starting to date again. He joined a popular Christian dating site and developed a profile that focuses on his desire to follow the leading of Jesus. He is struggling with the loss of his marriage after his wife had an affair. After the second date with a woman he enjoyed, she showed up at his apartment in a trench coat, and when he opened the door she pulled her coat back to reveal she was naked except for high boots. He stammered, closed the door, and drank a bottle of wine as he watched television that night.

It should be obvious that we live in a mad world that is sexually tinged and provocative in every media outlet, workplace, church, neighborhood, and home. We live in an increasingly sexual milieu that is progressively transgressing the boundaries of every sexual practice, including pedophilia. Miley Cyrus, in the now infamous Video Music Awards show, masturbates and performs simulated fellatio on her partner while wearing a bear costume. Her stage is filled with dancers wearing large teddy bears on their backs. The image couldn't be clearer: the symbol of childhood innocence, a teddy bear, is participating in the sexual emancipation of a child star, Hannah Montana, into the sexual freedom of a vamp.

It is not that Miley Cyrus is promoting pedophilia, but she is reveling in the power of transgressing childhood innocence, and that is similar to the desire of a pedophile. We live in a world where sexual desire seems anything but holy. Instead, it is bound to self-absorbed indulgence, transgression, and violence. To link holiness and sexuality seems like an oxymoron in our day. Yet this is simply the by-product of evil's desire to free sex from true spirituality and holiness.

This book defends two core assertions. First, sexual desire doesn't begin to be released on the altar the second after you say "I do." It begins in the womb and grows irregularly and progressively through our lifetime until death, and from childhood until death this journey is fraught with turns, twists, disasters, failure, and growth. Second, sexual desire is meant to become more holy and whole the longer we live. It is important to consider what it means to be holy and how that relates to sexual desire.

Holy, Holy, Holy

Holiness is a central and core description of the character of God. He is holy. All that he does is holy, and he requires holiness of those in his presence. What does it mean to be holy? There are three key elements to the meaning of the word. To be holy is to be set apart; to be without flaw, blemish, or stain; and to shine with a fire-like brightness, full of glory and awe. We are to be like God, set apart as his beloved; to be beautiful, without flaw or blemish; to be bright and shining in his sight, a blessing to him and to the world. All holiness involves being beloved, beautiful, and a bright blessing.

Set Apart: Chosen to Be His Beloved

To be holy is to grow in the awareness that we are God's chosen delight. We are a holy people, set apart for his pleasure. We are beloved, and we carry the mantle of his covenant commitment to show us favor in spite of our lust, anger, adultery, and murder. He has chosen us in Christ Jesus, and he can no more reject or discard us than he can reject or discard his beloved Son.

Holiness is not our achievement; it is a gift from our holy God. No one is sexually holy—married, single, gay, straight, or celibate—but we are gifted with holiness just as we are with faith. It is not our work but the gift of God. We must then approach the gift of sexual holiness with fear and trembling, knowing that our sin cannot cause us to be discarded, nor can it turn him from seeing us as his beloved. Just as salvation is a gift that must be worked out in fear and trembling, so is holiness.

Without Flaw or Stain: Arrayed to Be Beautiful

To be holy is to be without flaw, stain, or blemish. Evil desires for us to be sexually used and then discarded. It also works to make us feel dirty, fouled, and ruined. God's gift of holiness is the promise that he will clothe us in his most beautiful righteousness so that we are dressed to be stunning and arrayed in his beauty. What God increases in us through the gift of holiness is the desire for our sexuality to be caught up in wonder and joy. We are meant to long for our experience of nakedness and pleasure, to be freed from shame and made holy, good, and innocent.

Holiness is not reaching perfection in this life; it is the *desire* to be set aside (chosen), blameless (beautiful), and revelatory of his glory (blessing). No one is sexually perfect, and our stains, flaws, and failures are used by God to intensify our surprise and wonder and to increase our gratitude for how his perfect love cannot be thwarted by our imperfection.

Bright Fire: Called to Be a Blessing

The design of evil is for sex to be hidden in the dark, ignored, unspoken, and filled with disgust. Adam and Eve flee from their Creator to hide and cover themselves and then turn to contempt and disgust to further hide their shame.

Our sexuality is not to be hidden and held in institutional contempt by the systemic silence that shrouds virtually all discussions of sex in the church. Seldom is the joy of sex spoken of, nor is the sorrow of our brokenness.

Seldom is sexual sin normalized, nor is sexual joy spoken of as the height of what God longs to restore in salvation. Sex is, at best, viewed as a great benefit of being married, rather than as a gift for every human—married or not. We simply do not have the language or experience to talk about God's desire to bless sexuality as part of the universal experience of being human. And if we consider sexuality as a blessing in marriage, we have not gone beyond this awareness to consider how our sexuality is meant to be a blessing to everyone with whom we engage on a day-to-day basis.

Holiness grows as we surrender more and more to God's calling for us to be his—a beautiful bride—revealing through our brokenness the allure of his undeserved, unexpected, matchless love. We grow in our capacity to hold his glory and increase our heart's desire for him the more we are seized by the extravagance and lavish love of our beloved. Sex is about pleasure. It is about an intimate, exclusive, loyal bond that is beyond words and comprehension, but not outside what our mind and body can imagine and desire.

> Sex is about pleasure. It is about an intimate, exclusive, loyal bond that is beyond words and comprehension, but not outside what our mind and body can imagine and desire.

God intends to purify our desire in the holy consumption of his love. We must take the risk of bringing our desire—holy and impure before his eyes—to be caught up in what sex is meant to offer: the arousal of our deepest desire to be in union with him.

This book invites you to consider what it means to grow in the holy desire of being beloved, beautiful, and bright, and how our sexuality—holy and broken, beautiful and bent—is used by God to draw us deeper into his love.

1

Song of Songs

A Holy and Erotic Book

Is the Song Sexual or Spiritual?

Song of Songs is a collection of related erotic love poems that emphasizes the goodness of sex. It does not hesitate to arouse and entice, nor does it fail to warn and caution. It is a book that has been considered too dangerous to be in the canon or read by those new to the biblical message.

By far the most common reading of the text is to desexualize it by seeing it as an allegory of Christ and his church. As an allegory, the book is not about sex—heavens no!—but is a spiritual tale told through the apparently sensuous language of a marriage relationship. This presumes that each chapter develops the story toward an ending that, like any allegory, concludes with a lesson to be learned.

There are God-honoring folks who hold passionately to this position. We believe they are wrong. Not only does an allegorical approach rob the text of its true meaning, but it makes the Bible a book with magical meanings to be decoded by the expert. In fact, an allegorical approach steals from us one of the strongest messages that we need today: God loves sex.

Of course we live in a sex-crazed world. It is mad in terms of obsession with media (television, films, music, magazines) and mad in that sexuality is the subject of profound abuse, perversion, distortion, and violence as a normal course of life through pornography, prostitution, sexual abuse, human trafficking, rape, and promiscuity. But the church must deal with sex differently than it has historically. And the Song of Songs offers a fresh and lucid frame of reference to help us define what it means to be both sensuous and holy.

Unfortunately we are up against a long history of not telling the truth about the Bible's sexuality and our own. We live in a day in which people hide their struggles and pretend to live above the erotic fray, or confess their struggles and remain blissfully ignorant about the violence of their own desire.

As a therapist I (Dan) would love to collect a dollar for every time I have heard promiscuity explained away as "looking for love in all the wrong places." The problem in this case is one of blaming topography. "If only I had been in church instead of in a bar, then I wouldn't have been tempted to sleep with him/her." Sadly, the stories I have heard about misguided sexuality in the church by pastors, elders, youth directors, music directors, deacons, and congregants make most bars look far safer.

> The church must deal with sex differently than it has historically. And the Song of Songs offers a fresh and lucid frame of reference to help us define what it means to be both sensuous and holy.

The point is simple and disturbing: every human being on this earth struggles with sexual thoughts, feelings, and behaviors that are contrary to love and in conflict with the holiness of God. We can either pretend that a few struggle with sexual problems that don't tempt the rest of us, or we can openly acknowledge that all humanity is caught up in sexual wars that must be engaged if we are truly to be human.

We believe that sexuality has the potential to entrap our soul and body in lust and sexual harm, but we also believe that the God of the universe intends to redeem and revolutionize our sexuality so that we might know unfettered pleasure, not only with our spouse, but in relationship with our

God. Sex is not only sensual and physical; it is also profoundly personal and spiritual. To separate our sexuality from our spirituality is to rob both of meaning and passion. Holiness is not a flight from our body or an aversion to sensuality.

Song of Songs leads us in a new understanding of sensual holiness as long as we are not sidetracked by its two-thousand-year history of Christian neoplatonic de-eroticization. We do not benefit from extreme modesty, such as the fabled blushing Victorian covering of piano legs to keep tender souls from lusting. The Song is bawdy yet discreet, poetic and dense, arousing and erotic, honest and convinced of the primal impulse of love to rise against death.

We will approach the Song of Songs not as a progressive allegory but as a book of individual poems or songs. The Song is not ordered in a form that requires the reading of one poem as a precursor to reading the next. Therefore, we will approach the book looking at themes related to sexuality rather than poem by poem. Tremper will explain why this is a far more faithful reading of the text in the analysis sections of the book. The translation of the Song that we use is Tremper's from his commentary on the book.[1]

In addition, we will approach this poetic book through the use of fiction, by looking at a group of fictional characters in an imagined scenario. We desire that Christians will do more than merely alter their personal viewpoints about the nature of sexuality, our struggles, and the way of redemption. We want people to engage each other with honor and honesty about sexuality—in community and not merely in isolated, whispered conversations that can never fully get at what is binding our hearts or limiting our joy. Sexual harm comes through relationships, and sexual healing equally comes through the process of reclaiming our sexuality in relationship with our spouse and others.

What does that mean? What does it look like? There are so few people who have reflected on a redeemed sexuality that it requires imagination to envision a new future. Just as science fiction often presages and encourages technology that might appear decades later, so fiction—an imagined story—can point to what is possible if we begin a different way of being sexual in this world. Therefore, interspersed with formal analysis of the Song of Songs will be a story set in a fictional small group that is attempting to study the book together. The Bible study is made up of two couples, a single woman, a single man, and a woman who is separated from her abusive husband. The narrating voice of the fictional sections will be Malcolm, a twenty-six-year-old recent convert to Christianity who led a promiscuous life prior to coming to faith and is still not fully persuaded that Christians he has met are any less troubled or immoral than he was or is.

Where Did the Song Come From?

Listen to the first several verses of the Song of Songs.

> Let him kiss me with the kisses of his mouth,
>   for your love is better than wine.
> How wonderful is the scent of your oils;
>   your name is poured out oil.
> Therefore, the young women love you.
> Draw me after you; let's run!
>   The king has brought me into his bedroom. (1:2–4a)

What in the world is a passage like this doing in the Holy Bible?

This has been the reaction of many through the ages as they have read the Song's passionate expressions of an unnamed man's desire for physical intimacy with an unnamed woman and, as here, of the woman's desire for the man. Indeed, through much of history, the church has repressed the commonsense meaning of the book by means of an allegorical interpretation.

The Song was written during Old Testament times (we don't know exactly when), but even if it was among the last books to be included in the canon of the Jewish people (around 300 BC), it was still centuries before the first surviving written interpretation appeared. Indeed, the first voice we hear commenting on the proper way to read the Song comes from a rabbi named Akiba (AD 100), who has left us two memorable statements on the book. First, he said that "whoever sings the Song of Songs with a tremulous voice in a banquet hall and (so) treats it as a sort of ditty has no share in the world to come."[2] This statement tells us two things: people understood that the Song spoke of sex, and the religious authorities were doing their best to repress that meaning. Then, in response to those who felt that the Song should not even be in the Bible because of its sensuality, Akiba responded: "God forbid!—no man in Israel ever disputed about the Song of Songs [that he should say] that it does not render the hands unclean, for all the ages are not worth the day on which the Song of Songs was given to Israel; for all the writings are holy, but the Song of Songs is the Holy of Holies."[3]

Akiba gave the Song an exalted place because he believed that the book spoke not of the love between a man and a woman but rather of the love between God and his people. In other words, he did not read the Song according to the obvious, commonsense meaning of the words, but rather he discovered a figurative meaning by understanding the book as an allegory. In this understanding, the man is God and the woman is Israel. The Song of Songs, then, is the story of the relationship between God and Israel. If Akiba is correct, then Song of Songs is unquestionably the Bible's most intimate and passionate description of God's relationship with his people. We get glimpses of that sensual and intimate love in many passages (Hosea 2:14–20, for example), yet there is no single book in the Bible that makes that love the entire focus. No wonder Akiba considered the Song of Songs to be the holy of holies.

Over the next seventeen hundred years, till the mid-nineteenth century, most Jewish interpreters took this approach to the Song. For instance, the Targum to the Song, an interpretive Aramaic paraphrase of the book composed sometime between AD 700 and 900,[4] interpreted the woman's words quoted above (1:2–4a) as a reference to the exodus from Egypt. This makes sense when the book is understood as an allegory, since the woman, Israel, is asking the man, God, to take her into his bedroom (the promised land).

Early Christians learned this allegorical interpretation from Jewish teachers and changed it to fit their theology. For early Christian interpreters, the man was Jesus and the woman was either the church or the individual Christian.

> My lover is to me a sachet of myrrh
> lodging between my breasts. (1:13)

This is taken as a reference to Jesus Christ (the sachet of myrrh), who spans the Old and New Testaments (symbolically represented by the woman's breasts). As with Jewish interpretation, this type of reading was prominent among Christian interpreters until the mid-nineteenth century.

It is not difficult to imagine why the allegorical interpretation came to be the dominant paradigm: we are desperate to know that God loves us, and we are awkward in addressing our sexuality. This interpretive structure gives us a way of resolving both our hunger and our awkwardness.

So then, what happened in the mid-nineteenth century that caused Jewish and Christian interpreters to turn from an allegorical understanding of the book to one that recognized it as love poetry? We will briefly consider the factors underlying this shift.

The nineteenth century saw the beginning and development of archeological exploration of Israel and the broader Middle East, starting with Napoleon's invasion of Egypt. Seeing the pyramids and other monumental relics fired the imagination of Europeans, and they began sending scholars to the region, which led to the discovery of ancient writings. These ancient writings included love poetry. This love poetry sounded a lot like the Song of Songs, and it helped recover the understanding that the Song has to do with human love.[5]

Besides ancient love poetry, European diplomats in places like Damascus attended weddings of important Arab officials. They heard erotic songs at the ceremonies that reminded these biblically literate politicians of the Song. Many of these songs described the physical beauty of the bride and the groom in the manner of Song of Songs 4:1–5:1; 5:10–16; and 7:1–10. These songs were preludes to the lovemaking of the wedding night.

It thus became increasingly obvious that the Song of Songs was not an allegory, but rather that through the centuries an allegorical interpretation was imposed on it. An honest and impartial assessment of the book reveals that the Song bears none of the features of an allegory. After all, allegories are quite obvious, and the relationship between a feature of the story and its meaning is usually one to one. Take, for example, the most famous allegory of all, *The Pilgrim's Progress*. What is *Pilgrim's Progress* about? It is about a man named Christian who is traveling to the Celestial City. Along the way he encounters obstacles like the Slough of Despond. The symbolic meaning of this book is obvious, nothing like the Song of Songs.

If the Song is not an allegory, however, why did so many intelligent people read it as such for so many years?

The Limits of Self-Control

Looking back from the vantage point of the twenty-first century, we can clearly see how Jewish and Christian interpreters were deeply influenced by the culture of the day (as we are today). In particular, educated religious leaders were influenced by the philosophy of Plato, which pitted matters of the spirit over against the body. They reasoned that the body was a hindrance to the spiritual life. Thus, to grow spiritually the body had to be ignored—or worse. Thus we see the rise of a celibate priesthood and the emergence of the monastic movement from the early church through the Middle Ages and beyond.

To these Christians, nothing was more connected to the body than sex. But it was not only the physical act of sex that discouraged spiritual formation in their view; it was also the emotions that went along with it. Sex arouses intense desire—desire directed not toward God but toward the other. One can lose one's self-control and reason in the throes of passion.

This explains the behavior of many of the great theologians of the early church and their interpretation of the Song. Origen (AD 185–253/54), truly a monumental figure in the development of early Scripture interpretation, did to the Song of Songs what he did to his own body.[6] He castrated himself to keep from acting on his sexual impulses, and he "desexed" the Song by treating it as an account of the relationship between Jesus and the church rather than speaking about the physical intimacy of a man and a woman. Jerome (AD 331–420), another giant of the faith, used to throw himself into a thorn bush whenever he felt sexual arousal, so it is no surprise that he too adopted an allegorical approach to the Song. Indeed, in a letter to his disciple Paula concerning how she should direct her daughter in Scripture reading, Jerome said that she needed to read the whole Bible and even "commit to memory the prophets, the heptateuch (the first seven books of the Old Testament), the Books of Kings and of Chronicles, the rolls also of Ezra and Esther," before she could read the Song of Songs. For otherwise, "if she were to read it at the beginning, she would fail to perceive that, though it is written in fleshly words, it is a marriage song of a spiritual [wedding]. And not understanding this she would suffer from it."[7]

Approaching the Song with a belief that sex and its passions are at war with holiness encouraged these celibate interpreters to adopt an interpretive approach that, in essence, made the book say something different than what it obviously says. Much later, John Wesley (1703–91), the founder of the Methodist Church, illustrated this type of reasoning when he said, "The description of this bridegroom and bride is such as could not with decency be used or meant concerning Solomon and Pharaoh's daughter; that many expressions and descriptions, if applied to them, would be absurd and monstrous; and that it therefore follows that this book is to be understood allegorically concerning that spiritual love and marriage, which is between Christ and his church."[8]

The Invisible Book

Today, one looks in vain for a scholarly treatment—whether Christian (Protestant and Catholic) or Jewish—that would take the Song as an allegory in the manner of Akiba, the Targum, Origen, Jerome, or Wesley. However, the sexual meaning is often suppressed in the church today in one of two ways. Some pastors still teach and preach the Song as an allegory of the relationship between Jesus and the Christian, while ignoring its message concerning sex. However, most often the Song is repressed by ignoring it altogether. When was the last time you heard a sermon on the Song of Songs? Maybe it was read at a wedding, but a concerted focus on the Song is often missing from our churches and our Bible studies.

Indeed, I (Tremper) was once disinvited from preaching at a church because I chose as my text a passage from the Song. The pastor knew I was going to preach on the Song because he invited me to preach on Valentine's Day. When his elder board heard about it though, they forced him to cancel my invitation. Apparently there are parts of the Bible that are too radical to be treated in a sermon!

But such an attitude is not only cowardly; it is dangerous. By removing the Song from Scripture on a practical level—by not reading it, teaching it, or preaching it—we keep ourselves from clearly hearing God's voice on sex, and sexuality is a significant and often confusing part of our human experience.

If the Song of Songs is not an allegory and is in fact a collection of erotic love poems, then does it speak only of human sexuality and say little or nothing about our relationship with God? Far from it. Our central conviction, which we will explore throughout the book, is that sex is a window into the heart of God, pure and simple, even though our experience of sexuality is usually complex and tinged with the debris of the fall.

It is easy to see why some would prefer the Song of Songs to be solely spiritual or solely physical. It makes the book and our own experience of it less complicated. In fact, what is seen reveals the nature of what can't be seen. In Romans 1:20, Paul suggests

> By removing the Song from Scripture on a practical level, we keep ourselves from clearly hearing God's voice on sex.

that the visible makes known God's invisible character, and the implication of his claim is staggering. What does that imply about the body of a woman? A man? Their union and climax? The rise and fall of hormones before, during, and after intercourse? It compels us to ask the question: What is God's goal for sex? We can at least say that the pleasure and transcendence are not as separable as they might seem.

Today we mistakenly either separate sexuality and holiness by a huge chasm or merge them in a pantheistic, immanent unity. The church often makes sexuality unspiritual, just as the world substitutes a sexual encounter for a spiritual experience. We must find a way to embrace the uniqueness of our bodies and our spirits and experience the intersection not as a loss of one or both but as the fulfillment of each.

Drama or Collection?

As we have described, the interpretation of the Song has moved away from the idea that it is an allegory and toward the idea that it is love poetry. That said, the next question is, what type of love poetry? Is it a poetic drama that tells a single story, or is it a collection of different love poems similar to the Psalms?

Some readers wrongly believe that the Song is a drama. In other words, it tells a single story. The purpose of interpretation then is to discover and describe the story. The weakness of this approach is exposed by the different stories discovered by various interpreters. Indeed, those who take this approach to the book even disagree over whether there are two main characters in the book or three.

On the surface, the two-character approach appears promising, since it looks like there is one unnamed man and one unnamed woman who speak and interact in the book. Sometimes the man is identified as Solomon (mentioned in 1:1, 5; 3:7; 8:11) and the woman as the Shulammite (6:13). While there are many variations on this two-character approach to the book, the plot is usually said to follow the journey of their relationship as it moves from courtship to marriage to a honeymoon, followed by conflict and reconciliation.

However, other readers detect a third major character in the book. They accomplish this by insisting that there are actually two men, a king and a shepherd, in the book along with the woman. The three-character approach introduces an interesting twist: a love triangle. Again variations abound among those who take this interpretive approach, but the basic plot is said to concern a lustful king who tries to force an innocent country girl into his harem. She, however, virtuously maintains her love for the shepherd boy back home.

All of this makes for interesting reading and is born from an impulse readers have to see a story even where there isn't one. The fact that the advocates of a narrative reading cannot even agree about whether there are two major characters or three suggests that they are reading a story into the poems rather than discovering a story intended by the author.

This book will approach the Song as a collection of love poems rather than a single poem telling one story. We will explore the Song's themes by explaining the powerful and sensuous imagery and being sensitive to the poet's expressions of emotions. The Song is a collection of about twenty poems. They are individual poems to be sure, but there is still a type of literary (not narrative) coherence among them. A man and a woman speak throughout the book. They are not identified as specific people (more on this below), yet their voices (along with the supporting chorus, often called the "daughters of Jerusalem") provide a kind of consistency throughout the book. It is not that new poems introduce different characters. Rather, different poems deal with the same characters but do not tell a single, unified story.

In addition, the Song has a kind of coherence that is provided by two refrains that are repeated in the book. On two occasions, the woman says, "His left hand is under my head, and his right embraces me" (2:6; 8:3). Three times she utters, "I adjure you, daughters of Jerusalem, by the gazelles or the deer of the field, not to awaken or arouse love until it desires" (2:7; 3:5; 8:4). These and many other features give a sense that these multiple songs cohere into a single song. Perhaps this is one reason why the book is described in the first verse as a "song of songs."

This understanding of the Song of Songs explains why we will be treating individual poems out of their order as we explore the major themes of the book and asking how they shape our own perceptions, emotions, and behavior in matters of sexuality and spirituality. But, first, let's explore the book's main message to its readers. The Song is, first of all, a celebration of sex.

Most of the Song's poems celebrate sex. Notice that it is sex, not love, whose pleasures these poems praise. That is not to say, of course, that the physical intimacy desired and enjoyed by the man and the woman does not arise out of love; it certainly does. But with only one notable exception (8:5–7), that love is expressed as a yearning for physical touch. In the chapters that follow, we will examine poems that express desire (chap. 4), describe physical beauty (chap. 7), and depict sexual scenes (chap. 10), as well as express the glory of sex (chap. 16).

The Song is, first of all, a celebration of sex.

By far the most important message of the book is the celebration of sex, but an important minor theme must also be pointed out. Sex is so wonderful that the danger is to engage in a sexual relationship impulsively and prematurely. Thus, some of the poems are dedicated to warning that this wonderful gift is also fraught with danger and needs to be approached carefully. We will deal with these struggles of sexuality in chapters 12 and 13.

Who Are the Man and the Woman?

As we enter into the following chapters, it is important to identify precisely who the man and the woman are in the poems. Perhaps you will be surprised to learn that they are you! Let us explain.

The man and the woman are intentionally not made specific characters so that those married couples who read it can identify with the characters and can be inspired to speak sensuous words to one another. In other words, the Song of Songs is very much like the book of Psalms in this regard. While we might be able to identify an author of a psalm from the title (as in Ps. 51, which names David as its composer), the psalm itself speaks in the first person.

> Have mercy on me, O God,
>> according to your unfailing love;
> according to your great compassion
>> blot out my transgressions. (Ps. 51:1)

Notice that David does not embed the particular situation that inspired him to write the psalm (the title specifies his adultery with Bathsheba). This shows his intention not to memorialize his experience but rather to compose a prayer that can be used by later worshipers who have a similar though not necessarily identical situation.

The Song works the same way. Surely the poet expresses his own emotions but does so in a way that allows the reader to identify with them and learn from them.

But what about Solomon and the Shulammite? We mentioned above that Solomon and a woman who is given the name Shulammite are mentioned, though rarely, in the book. Aren't we to identify the man and the woman with them?

No, we are not. They play a different role. Shulammite is mentioned only once in the book. Solomon is mentioned a few more times, but he does not speak; he is spoken about. He also plays different roles in the book. The only substantial references to Solomon in the book are in 3:5, where his marriage is used to enhance the glory of weddings, and in 8:11, where he is an example of someone who tried to buy love.

That said, it is interesting that Shulammite is a feminine form of the name Solomon (which in Hebrew is *Shelomo*) and that both are based on the Hebrew root *shalom*, which means, among other things, "peace" or "contented." Perhaps we are to have in the backs of our minds the idea that the union of Shelomo and Shulammite would lead to contentedness. That contentedness is the consequence of physical intimacy and is, after all, the point of the poem in 8:8–10 (to be described in chap. 16).

The bottom line is that married couples benefit from reading this book together and placing themselves in the roles of the man and the woman.

Who Are the Daughters of Jerusalem?

Throughout the Song, we hear from and about a group of women who are sometimes identified as the "daughters of Jerusalem" (also sometimes called "daughters of Zion" or "women of Jerusalem"). They serve multiple functions in the poems of the book. Sometimes they are the disciples of the woman. They hear her and watch her and learn in the ways of love. They give third-person witness to the beauty and goodness of the relationship of the man and woman, acting at times almost like cheerleaders encouraging them in their intimacy (5:1). Other times they are the object of the woman's warning that such a passionate relationship should only be entered when the time is right (2:7; 3:5; 8:4). We will have more to say about these and other passages connected to the daughters in the following chapters.

The Brothers and the Mother

Some members of the woman's close family also play a role in this poem. Her mother never speaks but is mentioned in a couple of passages, including one particularly telling example in 8:2, when the woman says,

> I would lead you; I would bring you
>   to the house of my mother who taught me.

The passage then discreetly describes how the woman would lead the man into lovemaking. Thus, the mother is the one who has schooled her daughter in matters of love.

The brothers play an even more active role. They are spoken about in 1:5–6, and then they speak in 8:8–10. What unites these passages is the fact that brothers played an important role in marriage negotiations in ancient Israel. We can see this, for instance, in Genesis 34 where the brothers interact with Shechem, who wants to marry their sister. Again, we will wait till we treat these passages in chapter 13 to explore this in more detail.

The Poetry of the Song

Before looking at specific passages in the Song, we need to point out the obvious. It is poetry and needs to be read as poetry. What does that mean? First, poetry is compact language. It says a lot using very few words. We need to slow down and ponder poetry as we draw out its meaning. Second, we should expect not absolute clarity of meaning, but rather artful and intentional ambiguity in poetic language. The many powerful images speak indirectly, but truly.

It can almost be assured that poetry doesn't carry one single meaning. Or, said differently, it is not true that a rose in a poem means a rose is a rose. The word "rose" may refer to a flower we call a rose, but it could also be used to symbolize a woman whose beauty has captured the poet and has pierced him when he tried to take hold of her.

A modern reader's apprehension of the poem is also hindered by the fact that ancient images are sometimes less clear to us than they were to the ancient reader or listener. What does it mean to say that someone's eyes are "like doves" for instance (4:1; 5:12)? Does this refer to their color, their fluttering, or something else? We can't be sure. Poetic language must be respected for its powerful evocation of emotion and thought, but not pressed to say more than it intends to say.

Reading the Song in the Light of the Whole Bible

No book of the Bible should be read in isolation from the rest of the canon. While each book, including the Song, makes an individual contribution to the whole Bible, the ultimate context of a book is found as part of the entire canon. Reading the Song in the light of the rest of the Bible helps us understand the meaning and significance of the book according to its divine purpose, as we will explain in the following sections.

Marriage and the Song

There is a noticeable lack of explicit mention of marriage in the Song. Song of Songs 3:6–11 reflects on Solomon's wedding in a way that illustrates the glory of marriage. The erotic description of the woman finds the man referring to her as his "bride" in chapter 4, starting at verse 8, through chapter 5, verse 1, but otherwise there are few references to the fact that they are married.

However, to think that a book in the Bible celebrates the sexual intercourse of an unmarried couple is a mistake bred by reading it from a modern context outside of its canonical and cultural setting. Ancient societies in general did not smile on extramarital and premarital sex, and the teaching of the Bible (Old and New Testaments) is explicit in promoting sexuality within the context of the legal commitment of marriage.

This realization raises questions: Who should read the Song of Songs and how? Who was it written for? We already stated above that the Song's two main characters, the man and the woman, were unnamed so that married couples can put themselves in their place. The Song then helps the couple find a language of erotic love with which to speak to each other as a prelude to lovemaking. Today, as in the past, the language of love and intimacy is not easy to express. It makes us too vulnerable to each other. Today, too, the ethos of the church sometimes discourages eroticism even within marriage. The Song is a counter to this idea. Just as the Lord's Prayer is a model of prayer to help us learn how to pray, so the Song is a model of godly sensuality.

But what about others? Is it just for married lovers? What value does it have for singles? Singles should identify themselves with the "daughters of Jerusalem." They look on (not voyeuristically) as the woman enjoys intimacy with the man. The "daughters" serve as a community (both men and women) that learns through suffering and celebrating the vicissitudes of sexuality. It is a role that is difficult to describe or comprehend: cheerleaders, neophytes, chorus—all of the above. In some ways, it is an apprenticeship in sexuality without the risk of harm, though also without the benefits of direct participation.

It is not voyeuristic in that the "daughters" feel the joy and suffer the ups and downs for themselves and their "friends." Also, they (and we the readers) are invited to witness not the physical lovemaking but only the thoughts and emotions of the beloved. But their participation must be viewed as implying that sexuality, though private in the act, is not a taboo subject. Christians often fail by not talking about sex enough. Others fail when they trivialize sexuality through interactions that are crude and familiar.

The "daughters" are also given instruction. They are told to wait until the time is right. The assumption is that the time may very well come for them and that it is good to be discipled in these matters. The Song can be an agent of discipleship.

Besides this, all readers can benefit from the theological dimensions of the Song. These dimensions arise from a canonical reading, which makes evident both that the Song is the story of the already-but-not-yet redemption of sexuality and that our relationship with God is like a marriage.

Return to Eden

Reading the Song canonically takes us back to the Garden of Eden. In Genesis 2, Adam and Eve are in the Garden enjoying a harmonious relationship with God and with each other. The creation of Eve from Adam's side signals their equality and mutuality, and Adam's exultant song reveals his joy.

> This at last is bone of my bones
>   and flesh of my flesh;
> this one shall be called Woman,
>   for out of Man this one was taken. (Gen. 2:23 NRSV)

Soon after, we are told that marriage is defined as leaving one's parents to form a new primary loyalty to one's spouse, joining together through common experience and communication, and then finally becoming one flesh through the enjoyment of sexual intercourse (Gen. 2:24). In terms of the Song, the most relevant statement in Genesis 2, in the final verse of the chapter (2:25 NRSV), is that the man and the woman were "both naked, and were not ashamed." This nakedness symbolized not only a physical openness to each other but also an unabashed spiritual, psychological, and emotional exposure. They had nothing to hide.

The next chapter, however, narrates Adam and Eve's rebellion against God. They asserted their own moral independence by saying they would define what was right and wrong and reject God's definition. The effect was immediate. Because they broke relationship with God, they felt alienation from each other, made public by their need to now cover themselves up from each other. At the end of Genesis 3, Adam and Eve now wear clothes, no longer able to bear exposure.

> The underlying message is that sexuality is redeemed. It is possible to enjoy God's good gift of sex in spite of sin.

The Song describes the man and the woman back in the garden (many of the poems have garden settings) once again enjoying each other. The underlying message is that sexuality is redeemed. It is possible to enjoy God's good gift of sex in spite of sin. That said, the Song is still a very realistic book. It affirms the redemption of sex, but it also recognizes that it is an already-but-not-yet redemption. There are still obstacles and dangers connected to intimate exposure. In chapters 12 and 13 we will examine and explore the not-yet aspect of the Song's message.

God as Husband

Finally, we read the Song in the light of the Bible's extensive teaching that God is our husband.[9] In the Old Testament, Yahweh is pictured as the husband of Israel. Unfortunately, most of the time the image is used negatively. Israel is God's wife, but she has committed adultery by worshiping other gods. Here we see the ground of the divine-human marriage metaphor. Relationship with God and marriage are the only two exclusive relationships. In the creation ideal, one can have only one spouse and only one God. To have more than one is a transgression against the relationship; thus there is an analogy between idolatry and adultery. While this negative portrayal of the divine-human relationship is found throughout the Old Testament, classic texts of this negative relationship are found in Ezekiel 16 and 23, and in Hosea 1 and 3.

That said, we do find glimmers of the positive use of the image, even if only as a reminiscence of better days gone by.

> I remember the devotion of your youth,
>   your love as a bride,
> how you followed me in the wilderness,
>   in a land not sown. (Jer. 2:2 NRSV)

> Therefore, I will now allure her,
>   and bring her into the wilderness,
>   and speak tenderly to her.
> From there I will give her her vineyards,
>   and make the Valley of Achor a door of hope.
> There she shall respond as in the days of her youth
>   as at the time when she came out of the land of Egypt.

. . . And I will take you for my wife forever; I will take you for my wife in righteousness and in justice, in steadfast love, and in mercy. I will take you for my wife in faithfulness; and you shall know the LORD. (Hosea 2:14–15, 19–20 NRSV)

The Song is not an allegory but is about marriage, and the more we learn about marriage, the more we learn about our relationship with God.

Themes

We will approach the poetry of the Song of Songs by looking at themes that arise throughout. These themes show up not only in the Song but in every person's sexual experiences.

Desire. How is it we come to desire our lover? How does desire invest, move, and transform us in a way that leads to love and not merely to lust? And what do we do with the reality that so many of our sexual desires are contrary to what we know is honoring and beautiful? For some, desire is a lust for taboo experience in one's marriage, and for others, sex is the price of admission or continuation of the marriage, something to be endured and not a passionate and pleasurable part of the process of lovemaking.

Erotic Triggers. What turns up the erotic heat at one point of the relationship may not do so a year later. Erotic arousal is variable and yet has some universal dimensions that are related to our biological differences. It is imperative to understand and to engage arousal as a part of us that is not all good or simply neutral. We can be aroused by triggers that are linked to past harm or to doing harm to others. We are aroused by series of images, symbols, or narratives to the point of sexual satisfaction for both husband and wife. Our body's arousal is connected to the individual images and stories that are bound to our sexual identity. What are the images and stories that are most honored and blessed in the Song?

Sexual Scenes. The poetry of the Song sets the scene for seductive teasing, verbal banter, setting up a tryst, dealing with privacy, preserving honor, and imagining the process of pleasuring one another. It uses holy and luscious imagery to set the scene for good sex. How are we to take from other nonbiblical narratives and poetry the erotic power of imagination without being defiled or defiling others in a form that is bawdy and pornographic?

Sexual Struggles. No one ever on this earth has been able to escape sexual wars. We are sexual beings from the day we are born to the day we die, and throughout our life we will struggle to know and embrace goodness in our sexuality rather than loss, shame, and contempt. How do we engage the heartache—past, present, and future—woven into our sexuality and still delight in what God has made for our pleasure?

> Sex is the one act that stands most opposed to the ravenous decay and destruction of death.

Glory of Erotic Faithfulness. Sex is far more than periodic ecstasy or—on a more mundane level—a romp that leads to brief and fleeting pleasure. A transcendent view of sexuality means that sex is revelatory, both in its parts and as a whole, of something greater than itself or the process. As we will see in more detail, sex is our best means to deal with the ever-present fear and loss that comes with death. Sex is more than procreative or relationship-building;

it is vastly more than mere sensuality and play. It is the one act that stands most opposed to the ravenous decay and destruction of death.

Our desire is to invite you to the intersection of your sexual desire, struggles, and search for the "more" that lingers in and about sexuality like a compelling fragrance. To the degree that we enter these turbid waters, we will discover the depths of our fear, heartache, harm, and fury as lived through one of the most intimate acts known to humanity. It is that ground that God intends to light up with his holy delight to redeem our sexuality.

Stay with us through this book and you will find yourself singing this resurrection sex song.

2

Roped In

I slammed the door to Agnes, my ancient Volvo, and the sound seemed even tinnier in the suburbs than outside my downtown condo. *What am I doing here?* I wondered. *What am I doing in the burbs?* Going to a Bible study on sex. Crazy. Why did I accept my boss's invitation to a group study on something called the Song of Songs? Apparently it's hot poetry or something in the Bible about sex. A study on sex from the Bible with five people I don't know, and the only one I do know can fire me. A bad idea, a really bad idea.

How did I get myself into this? Maybe it started when I met my boss's wife, Jill. Christmas party last year. Little black dress, pearls, and the Miu Miu sassy black shoes with the perky bow. It was just chance that I knew the designer's name. I had been shopping before Christmas with the girl I was dating, and she showed me a pair of shoes she hinted I might want to consider buying as a present. I picked up the shoe, and the pair cost over $500. I said, "I wouldn't buy that even for my wife or my mistress, even if I had just gotten a one-hundred-thousand-dollar bonus."

Her mouth turned downward and she sucked in her lips, an indication there wouldn't be any sex tonight.

She knew I couldn't afford the gift, but she wanted me to coo and purr about how sexy she would look in those shoes and tell her that I wished I had the money to buy her what she wanted. I knew the drill. I was just tired of it; I didn't want to earn sex by shopping with her, let alone coo for sex I knew I could get whether I worked for it or not.

But the name Miu Miu stuck in my head. How could it not? And when I said to Jill, "Oh, I love your Miu Miu shoes," she smiled coyly.

"Fashionista? How did someone who knows haute couture get into the world of heavy equipment?"

I wondered the same. I graduated four years ago with a degree in religion and philosophy, and somehow it prepared me to write copy and eventually sell fire engines for Stephen and Sons.

What did I know about fire engines? Nothing. What did I know about sales? Try too hard to score—whether with a woman or a customer—and you've lost the game. Give the play away by showing what you want and you lose. Better to invite them into the game with a little self-deprecation and let them think they are directing the seduction. Score!

But that was the problem. It was all a game I'd learned to play long ago, even with my mom, and I was tired, sick to the bone of getting through the door to find the room sensually arousing but empty. Not empty because my current affair was there, but rather just vacant because I was as hollow as a sound studio. My recent conversion, if that is what it is called, to Christianity is due to my boss and my dubious fortune to have seduced a girl who gave me a book by Kierkegaard. What a freaking riot. I am a Christian because I got tired of sex.

"I am a Christian." The sound of those words is haunting. I'm glad I haven't told many people because it may not last any longer than it did for Bob Dylan.

How could I know the comment about Miu Miu shoes was going to get me into such trouble? We talked and I think flirted for about ten minutes before my boss, Marty, came up to assess what trouble his wife was causing.

"Marty, I just love your new hire. It's refreshing you've hired someone other than a mechanical troglodyte. How did you get the sense to hire a really smart kid?"

I winced at the word "kid" but figured it was a safer reference than "stud."

I am twenty-six, and even in the last decade no one has considered me a stud or a ladies' man. It is easier to fly below the radar waves and hit one's target than to have a reputation that makes women leery or suspicious. A number of women were intrigued by my under-the-radar approach, at first wondering if I was gay. At six foot two I am tall without being imposing. My hair is brown and longish and falls easily behind my ears. A girl I once dated said, "I love how you push your hair behind your ears, as if even your hair is shy and not sure whether to hide or hang out."

I was caught off guard by her remark. I feel shy. I am far more comfortable with women than men. If I have to read about sex in the Bible, I'd rather read it alone at home than chat about it with a bunch of Christians in a Bible study.

And seriously, what does the Bible have to say about sex? That's what got me into trouble with Jill. Marty told Jill, "Now don't monopolize his time. I want him to mingle and get to know some of the employees he hasn't met yet." I knew I was being watched. And it was obvious that we were flirting.

"Marty tells me that you have recently become a Christian."

"True. This me and Jesus thing is kind of a big surprise. I spent most of my life as a nominal Episcopalian, and religious fervor or commitment is seen as a sign of imbalance if not derangement."

"You're funny. Well, whatever brought you to Christ I'm happy to be your older sister in the Lord. If there's anything we can do to help you, to be part of your growth, I hope you'll let us know. Oh, speaking of, after the New Year, probably early February, we'll be hosting a Bible study taught by a friend of ours. Would you be interested in coming?"

"Well, I have never been part of any Bible study. I always thought that meant Bible scholars poring over ancient manuscripts and making colorful charts and calligraphy. So you and others study the Bible together?"

"Oh how fun! You really are new to Jesus, aren't you?" Before I had a chance to answer, she put her hand on my arm. I could feel her long, strong fingers kneading my arm like I was dough in her hands. It felt eerie, familiar, and good. I'd have gone to her room for any number of thrills. Or for a Bible study. It didn't matter. I was impaled then, on her red, manicured nails.

And then there I was walking into her house to study the Bible.

The living room felt like it belonged to a successful business owner—wingback chairs, a comfortable couch, a love seat adjacent to the couch, and an array of pillows for floor sitting. Seven showed up for the first study. Jon and Celeste were the appointed teachers.

Soon into the first meeting Jon said, "Celeste and I are like guides who have visited this country a few times prior to this trip and read a bit about the land, the people, and the history, but we are no more natives than you. We will study this book like a new country—reading and talking with each other to get the lay of the land, and perhaps, with some effort, we'll come to love what we read and allow this trip to transform us."

I laughed. It was rude, but I was taken aback by the thought we were going to take a road trip into sex.

I remember being sixteen and on my first road trip. We had left to go to Fort Lauderdale for spring break like all the kids from the frozen Midwest. I was with the parents of my best friend, and we were going to party in the sun, tan ourselves to a crisp, and sneak a few beers from my friend's older sister. She was twenty and in college. It was my first time to drink myself stupid, and that night I happened to walk to the beach alone, where I found the girlfriends of my friend's sister smoking pot. I sat down with them, the little brother, the kid, and we talked, laughed, and got high.

I don't remember when it happened, but I had been talking to one girl, Jamie, and she kept running her fingers through my hair. I wanted to puke. I was so scared I could cry, but she eventually turned my head toward her and kissed me. She kissed me long and deep. I felt my body shiver. She felt it too, and laughed. She pushed me back in the sand and that night began my decade-long experience of seducing and being seduced, of being touched amid laughter and play. The warmth of moist words and touch, the uncertainty and expectancy, the arousal, the slow and inevitable movement toward a completion that if it could only last longer might transform me, but in its inevitable brevity and incapacity left me feeling raw, naked, and used. And here I am now in the suburb's womb hearing we are going to take a journey to a foreign country to be transformed by sex. I have already been on that journey and am hoping to arrive at a different destination.

The whole group turned to look at me—the guy who just laughed for no apparent reason. Marty laughed too with a booming basso thunder. He was impossible not to notice. He was six foot four and married to Jill, a diminutive bundle of contradiction whose quiet presence barely hid her volatility.

Jon's face was warm and relaxed. He smiled and said, "Don't be too troubled by him, folks. Malcolm is new to the faith and will help us stay as real as we can be in this study."

I stifled a yawn. I had drawn about as much attention to myself as I could endure. I looked around the room, and next to Jon was Celeste. Jon was a middle-aged runner whose body was toned without looking overly buff. He was quietly handsome. Celeste had short, sleek blond hair. Her short hair revealed a thin, elegant, strong neck. She looked ten years younger than Jon, who had to be in his early fifties. She glowed. I had a hard time not staring. She smiled when I laughed out loud, and looked down as if she was embarrassed, but her eyes were full of life. Her eyes were dark, swift waters that hinted at what I suspected was more than merely good humor.

Next to me on the love seat was Lois. I was glad that I couldn't see her face without turning my head. Her face was pale yellow with blotches of red around her neck. She scared me. I suspect she may have been in her forties, but I wouldn't have been surprised to learn she was eighty. I remember the smell of my grandmother before she died—gardenias. Lois didn't smell like a gardenia, but I was curious why she didn't. Her neck was thick with flesh. When she turned to look at Jon, it continued to move after her head stopped. She sagged with age and bitterness.

We were invited by Jon to tell a few things about ourselves and to say why we were there and what we hoped to gain by a study of the Song of Songs. Lois stared long out the window into the dark, well-lit night. "I don't know. I wouldn't be here unless Celeste had bent my arm to come. I am separated from a man who physically hurt me, and I am not really fond of sex. I don't really want to believe it's God's plan, so I'm not sure if it's best for me to be here."

I wanted to agree, but not for the reason she expressed. I just didn't want to think of having to look at her for the next ten weeks.

Across from me on the pillows were Jill and Amihan, a single Filipino woman in her midthirties. Amihan scared me too. Early on in my first encounters with pornography I was aroused by any show of flesh by any women, young or old. Over time my habits became more addictive and demanding, and I found that I needed more compelling fantasies to keep aroused. Asian women had become mysterious to me, unknowable. I wanted that kind of woman and didn't want to look too directly in Amihan's eyes for fear that she would see that I had used women like her for a long time. So I smiled and thanked God that I was a decade younger and therefore wouldn't be expected to get together with her after the study.

"Any questions?" Jon asked. I had not even been aware he was talking. Apparently he had summarized his points, and I had missed both the first round and the summary. I only hoped no one would notice. I spend most of my life hoping that people won't notice that I am not paying attention.

Celeste said, "Really there are only four rules we'd ask for you to honor. Open your heart to God regarding your past and present struggles with sexuality. We've all suffered and sinned. We are all victims of past sexual struggles and active participants in a war that often defines and marks our identity. It's so important for us to submit our bodies and hearts to God through this study."

I tried to look attentive and sincere. We are all marked? I know I am, and I for sure know that Lois is littered with debris of some sort, but the rest? I smiled.

Want to do a quick truth or dare? I thought. I had no doubt that my life was darker than any of theirs, but what idiocy to be proud that I had more sexual activity. I'm proud that I could win in trading on sexual stories? In some sense, yes. I feel proud, or at least powerful. But not really. Actually I feel scared.

Celeste continued, "And second, we will divide our time each week between what the Bible says and then what it provokes in us." She paused and looked at her husband.

Jon added, "None of us knows what we are doing, really. I've never heard of anyone studying this book in a mixed group with two couples and three singles. So, we are going to have to improvise and see where God takes us. All we know is that it is best, in fact, a group rule, that we don't feel any pressure or expectation to share a single event, memory, or fact, whether from our past or present. This isn't a therapy group. It is a Bible study that intends to open our hearts to one another and to the Sex Song in the Bible. What happens must honor God. If you feel pressure to share, it is yours, not an expectation of the group. If you do share, we are not capable of counseling you or going further than thinking with you about the implications of your story and what we are reading. Everyone okay with that?"

All the heads nodded too quickly. What was I going to say? "Hey, I plan to pour out my sexual history like a jigsaw puzzle and I'm hoping you sincere, naive, and holy people will look at each sordid piece and come up with a picture of Jesus dining at the Last Supper." The thought made me laugh again. Suddenly, all the faces were looking at me expectantly.

"Sorry, I sometimes let my mind go, and for some reason I was thinking of that classic painting of Jesus serving his disciples at a meal."

Lois turned. "Really? How is that possible? How could a painting pop into your mind when we were talking about the group rules?"

"I know. Sorry. I guess I have lapses of attention." I heard her mumble, and I didn't want to know what she said. I could feel my pulse thicken. Her neck had patches of crimson beginning to coagulate in spider webs. I could count her pulse in one of the thicker veins on the left side of her neck.

Jon laughed. "Malcolm, if you space out, or go deep out to left field, or whatever, we are still fine with you being here."

I saw Lois squirm. Her abrupt questions seemed not to work, and I felt happy that Jon had shut down the old bat from flying up my nose.

Then he said to the group, "The third rule is this: Listen to the temptations, tensions, doubts, fears, shame, or whatever that arises as we go through this material. You will find it most helpful to keep a journal through this time. I'd encourage you to write soon after we leave, tonight if possible. Write about whatever comes to the surface. Just write, and write without editing or worrying that someone is going to find your journal. If you want, burn it the next day, or at the end of the study.

"Finally, everything that we talk about in this group must be kept 100 percent confidential. Nothing from our sharing is meant to be talked about with anyone outside of this group, even if it is clothed in the 'need for prayer.'"

And so, this, my first journal entry, officially one hour and twenty minutes after the end of the group, is done. We will see if there are any more entries. I'm not sure I can get away with not coming, and I am certainly not sure I can show up and talk about sex with the likes of this group.

3

Before the
Bible Study on Desire

am grounded in Modesto. The meeting with the buyer went smoothly, and I thought I'd be able to get out of town on the next plane. Not so.

I've been staring at the three vending machines that inhabit this third-world airport for four hours. San Francisco is closed to business pending a shift in the wind, or fog, or whether the political pack of wackos there decide to outlaw Happy Meals. It feels that capricious or random as to whether I will be allowed to leave Modesto. I am a little bit clearer how K felt in Kafka's *Trial*. On trial, judged, and condemned, yet still not knowing the crime.

I may be sentenced to this purgatory because I smirked. I was listening to the conversation between a middle-aged woman and her slightly younger male consort. They were chitchatting about the heat, the cost of bottled water, and the likelihood of the Angels getting some player for less than thirty million dollars. Then came the question from the man, "Are you from Modesto?"

"Yes, lived here my whole life. Love this place. It is near nirvana. Far enough from the smog and crime to feel safe and big enough that I don't care what my neighbor is doing. We've got a great deal."

He laughed. "What do you all grow or what is the industry here?"

She said, "Amonds."

"Amonds, not almonds?"

"We say 'amonds' around here because you have to shake the *L* out of them to get them to fall."

I stared at them until she caught my eye, then I smirked. She saw it and seemed happy that an obvious city boy felt superior to her country humor. She likely drew the conclusion that I was a liberal, had previously voted for Obama, wore Toms, and smoked the largest crop grown in California.

Or that I used to inhale and now don't. Pot is one of those things that slipped away once I got into this faith thing. It used to be the inhalant that took the edge off the irritating nasality of human beings. People were more tolerable and interesting if I was just slightly off-kilter. If I had been stoned I'd have laughed at the image of the *L*-less nut. I could see the town sweating in a community-wide celebration while shaking down the nuts to the sound of James Brown. But now I just got out-smirked by a bumpkin who saw through me. Normally, I am far better at the slow, salacious flirtation entailed in winning an older woman to my desire. I am off my beaten track.

I felt a text rattle my phone. It was from Jon.

Hey, Sex Song Gang . . . forgot to give you an assignment for our next meeting. We're going to start off with the topic of desire. Think about and do some writing on what feels good, bad, and ugly about sexual desire and what it would mean for you if God were first and foremost your most central desire, sexually and otherwise. See you on Wednesday. Jon

Have I lost my mind? I am going to talk about sexual desire with others in a Bible study. This is more bizarre than the fantasy of scantily clad Modestoites shaking the *L* out of almonds. What am I supposed to say? "Pot was my way of loosening the tension of living with people." "Sex allowed me to lose myself in another person and for an instant escape how small I felt."

That will go over famously. Better simply to confess that I like long or short legs, or big or petite breasts. "Are you a leg or breast man? Care for white or dark meat?"

This is insane. What am I supposed to say in a Bible study about my sexual desire?

Sex. I remember thinking when I was a kid that sex was about an orgasm. That was before ten thousand times of masturbation with the same, or nearly the same, fantasy. In fantasy, as in real life, if I knew we were going to have sex, then the thrill was over.

Sex was then really about desire. I suppose it is the adolescent craving to have power and access to someone whom we want that we know we can't have. Then we find we can have them, and the thrill of the chase is over.

Eventually I realized that not only had desire not gone away, but it had gone deeper. Desire was not fulfilled by the uncertainty and quivering hope of the chase. The deeper desire was still not for an orgasm—in fact, that was the finish, the small death that ended the dance. Sweet, quick, intense, finished. All that effort and all the aftermath of the relationship for a five-second burst . . . no one is that crazy. No one is crazy enough to risk AIDS for an orgasm! Not when it is so easily accomplished on one's own. There has to be more to sexual desire than sex. And that is what I am supposed to talk about with near-strangers in a Bible study? What the L—I can never say this stuff to the Bible study, but at least I can write it.

Most vacations are not for the taking, but for the planning and remembering. I don't really like to travel for fun. On the other hand, traveling for work is okay. At least the trip is paid for and the itinerary is clear. I know why I am here and what I need to do to be successful.

Mostly I need to remember the small facts about my client's kids, his pet peeves with his wife, and how his favorite teams are doing. It's not rocket science.

Sales is seduction and seduction is paying attention to the details, incidental details that tell the story that is most important to the buyer. No one really cares if I sell a Crimson Spartan Rescue Pumper or a Kenworth Pierce 4×4 Pumper Tanker. People don't buy on the basis of quality or cost; they buy because someone listened to and remembered their stories. The same is true with sex.

When I travel for "fun," I stare at a bridge, or eat at a famous restaurant and pay more money for the name than the sushi. I wander streets and meet up with friends who introduce me to sisters, work associates, and drinking partners. We talk. We laugh. We kibitz, flirt, weigh the options, and then drink slightly too much to make sex less adversarial. But it is always movement from talking to taking. And sex for me is finding room with another so that I don't have to sleep alone.

The problem is not about being awake and alone. I don't want to sleep alone. But sex is a huge price to be able to share another person's bed. It's like the sale. I won't keep my job if I don't get people to sign the contract. But it isn't the signing that thrills me. It thrills me about the same length of time as an orgasm—five seconds. It isn't even the chase to get the sale—the long, gaming seduction. I am mostly beyond that adolescent rush. I know in most cases the sale will occur, with someone, sometime. Persistence pays the dividend of relative certainty.

The desire is not in the planning—it simply doesn't take that much time or effort today to get laid. It isn't the memory after so many years. Remembering only intensifies the wound that needs to be stanched by more sex. Sex is the desire to forget and to dream only the present moment. As best as I can understand my turgid desire, all I want is flesh to hold onto as the gale winds strive to push us apart. Sex is an anchor that ties me to another human being long enough so that I can forget how silly life is. And it is.

Most conversations are simply chatter. Pleasantries. Or you can try the pale dusty trail of petty cynicism and sarcasm. We all seem to be little more than flesh eaters dining on banality or brutality. Sex is both, but at least without words. It is flesh penetrating flesh; flesh opening up to swallow flesh. It is a dance like children's parallel play where soundless fantasies get enacted without having to expend the effort to know what the other is thinking. Sex is real, yet doesn't have to be spoken to be experienced. It is at least some kind of relationship, and words will inevitably ruin it. Would that the world just be the rocking bliss of sensual fantasy—but instead, we fools seek not only for sex, but also for meaning.

What am I supposed to say to this sex Bible group? Do I tell them that I am not that fond of orgasms, but that they are inevitable and actually end the bliss? "What I want is to rock in the fantasy that I am locked into someone and for a few minutes we are stuck tighter than glue, inseparable and utterly interdependent, lost in pleasure to anything other than the silent movement of speechless grace."

Not likely. The desire for that kind of union wouldn't sell in *Playboy* or at a Billy Graham crusade. It just doesn't sell. No one will buy it—at the moment, not even me.

As crazy as all those words sound, what do I tell them regarding desire? Do I tell them I like older women? Not slightly older—I mean decades older. And when every man in the room looks at me as a threat and every older woman is offended and intrigued, do I salve their fears and tell them about my babysitter when I was six, or the older girls in our neighborhood who liked to play dolls with me and then practice making babies?

Not likely. The abuse card gets played by every celebrity and mass murderer. Even if it is true, it is too well worn a path for this cynic to walk. Or do I tell them that for the most part I hate my desire and wish it were dead? I can dally with it, occasionally feed it and put it to sleep, but what I can't do is either escape it or find anything good in it.

I know I can get married. I know I can remain single and remain mostly celibate with occasional lapses, or settle for serial monogamy in or outside marriage. But what I don't believe is that desire is anything less than a wraith that beckons to destroy. It is the hunger that makes us all cannibals even if we sit in proper attire, smile, and discuss the most recent Coen brothers release. I am so tired. But hark, I hear the nasal, monotone voice announcing that we trammeled souls are about to be released from purgatory. Time to board and pretend I never got that text.

4

The Dance of Desire

The Song of Songs is, among other things, a book about desire. Physical intimacy begins with desire. Desire is the fuel that propels a person to a dance of erotic play and pleasure. Desire serves to awaken the sleeper to move toward the sensuality of sexual engagement—it enables us to overcome hesitations borne of fear or of vulnerability and to seek union.

Desire is more than a drive or a craving. It is the sinew of sexuality that strengthens our arousal through sweet memory and keen anticipation. Or not. For many, sexuality is soiled with such hurt that desire is stifled—bound to memories of misuse and shame or disappointment and anger.

Desire for sex is not the same as the desire for intimate union. Nor is physiological arousal the same as a subjective desire for sex.[1] This division would have been inconceivable in an undivided, innocent, sin-free world. There the desire for sexual pleasure would have been entirely bound to the desire to arouse, bless, and serve the other—including through one's own body's pleasure. But we live in a world of difference where for women the presence of sexual desire or even arousal is not necessarily an indication of a desire for sex, though it could be, and for men sexual desire is more directly connected to sexual activity.[2] It is also a world of divided and distorted desire that wreaks havoc with every legitimate and holy longing.

Desire in a fallen world is seldom (if ever) untainted. Sexual desire, in particular, is layered with a legion of experiences that shadow even loyal and loving sex. One aspect of the struggle with desire concerns its intensity and orientation. The first issue for most couples is the differing degree of intensity of desire. For some, desire droops like a becalmed sail. It sags, and any movement comes through external duty or demand. For others, conversely, desire blows so strong that the sails are in danger of being overwhelmed and ripped. The demand for sex becomes a consuming passion that extinguishes thought or care until satisfaction is reached. The variance between luffing and burgeoning sails can be tragic and profound. Thankfully most people live somewhere between those extremes. It would be a mistake to assume that the two descriptions are gender divides with women falling into the former category and men into the latter. In fact, when it comes to sexual desire, though there may be differences in what elicits and evokes it for men and women, the levels of desire and even liking sex may not be as different as it has culturally been portrayed.[3]

> Desire is the fuel that propels a person to a dance of erotic play and pleasure.

However, desire between two lovers seldom pulses at the same volume before, during, or after sex.[4] A man can have desire for sex and yet not have erectile capacity, and a woman can be physiologically aroused and not have a subjective feeling of desire. The difference in desire is related to but not fully explained by gender, age, and unique history. We simply don't tend to follow with equal intensity the exact path of desire as anyone else.[5]

Mirroring desire and dealing with the dance of variance are as crucial to good sex as any single factor. In fact, most marriages never address desire outside of complaint.

"You want too much, too often."

"You never want to have sex."

"You don't want to try anything new."

Desire can't weather the steady drip of accusation and disappointment without eventually either dying or turning to another lover.

It is difficult to name one's desire or to hear one's spouse articulate what they want without succumbing either to accusation or guilt. We often coat ourselves with blame or feel suffocated by shame instead of simply hearing and receiving the desires of the other. Desire is not meant to become a demand, nor is it intended to merely fade away like footprints in the sand. Desire is meant to awaken us to be alert and attentive to the other, honoring their desire, but in a way that also honors one's own desires and sense of self.

A second issue with desire is orientation. The word in our day usually marks the difference between heterosexuality and the other orientations represented by the abbreviation LGBT (lesbian, gay, bisexual, transgendered). The problem with this distinction is that it doesn't do justice to the far wider range of objects of desire that is possible in the realm of sexual desire. We use the term "orientation" here to speak of the object or person of desire that most deeply sets into motion arousal and sustained behavior that moves toward sexual climax.

For example, a man can be heterosexually oriented but unable to be significantly aroused by his spouse. Instead of being aroused by her smile, fragrance, and the move of her head, he is primarily aroused by the fantasy of her in a girl's private-school uniform. Sex with a fully adult woman whom he engages emotionally with depth and richness through the terrain of life is not as enticing. When he wants sex, he draws on pornographic images he has culled through the years of undressing a thirteen-year-old schoolgirl. As dark as this is, it is not uncommon for both spouses to have someone other than each other in their hearts when making love. Our orientation is seldom full-faced toward the light of God.

The word "orient" derives from the idea of turning toward the east. The east is the direction from which the sun rises and from which we gain the first rays of light and warmth—it is our beginning point. Every person and every marriage has a sexual orientation; it is not a matter of simple choice. Sexuality is always a multilayered, multidimensional story. Our sexual desire begins with our first erotic impulses as we self-soothe by masturbating in the womb. Therefore, we come into this world primarily aware of the erotic pleasure that decreases stress and tension. Nothing settles emotional storms like masturbatory self-soothing. The intrauterine child or newborn doesn't understand the concept or experience of masturbation; it is simply hardwired in us for relief.

We enter the world erotically endowed in full and designed for arousal, pleasure, and union—to be satisfied not merely through genital stimulation, but through the provision of care and delight. It is easy to measure sexual health in terms of consistent genital satisfaction, as can be seen by the number of drugs available that are meant to enhance erectile function, with much research regarding sexual dysfunction for men being within the realm of genital performance. However, for women the experience of sexual satisfaction is based not solely on genital arousal but on factors that include the intersection of desire and connectedness to their partner.[6]

Through our childhood and into our adult years we enter into countless relationships that provide interpersonal paradigms for inciting excitation and providing satisfaction and *shalom*. This multitude of interactions provides us with building blocks for the development of our sexual orientation. Simply said, the greater the violation of God's paradigm throughout our life journey, the deeper the struggles with issues of intensity and orientation.

God's creation of sexual desire is far more than merely an evolutionary desire to propagate the species or achieve orgasm. Sexual desire intersects the poetic awakening of Adam to his female counterpart, Eve, and propels us to the last sentence in the creation narrative that speaks of a world without sin: "Adam and his wife were both naked, and they felt no shame" (Gen. 2:25 NIV).

Sexual desire is the physical prompting to move toward a pleasure that aches to escape division, loneliness, or shame. Sexual desire is not so much the desire for orgasm as it is the desire to be caught up in the sensuality of beauty that transcends the here and now for a timeless, undivided, unsoiled innocence. All other dimensions of lesser or distorted desire that we call sexual are cheap counterfeits or, far worse, a conscious effort to evade the Creator's design or transgress the Creator's boundaries.

The tragedy is that no one holds fully to the true east as we journey in our sexuality from birth to death. We are far, far more troubled and broken sexually than we are apt to confess. Certainly, our unique story of sexual development is far more complex and mysterious than to suggest there is a preordained, right path that if followed removes all or most complications. I (Dan) have worked with countless men and women who were virgins at marriage, escaped the perversion of pornography, and never kissed their spouse until their wedding day—yet still warred with dark desires or the absence of desire at various periods in their marriage.

There is no foolproof route to sin-free desire. Are we then hopeless and bound by whatever forces have made us who we are sexually? The promise of the Song is that love has the final word over all forms of death, distortion, or degradation.

> The promise of the Song is that love has the final word over all forms of death, distortion, or degradation.

Consequently, it is imperative to listen carefully to every desire that seems to rule our heart. Sadly, we have many desires that are contrary to God's design, and we are apt to indulge and then feel shame. Seldom do we listen and look courageously at our broken sexual desire and feel the kiss of God's delight.

A man I worked with could only experience sexual pleasure with his wife as he fantasized about his mother's shoes. As broken as this sounds, his desire was for an uncomplicated relationship with his wife, and his mother was viewed as the paragon of womanly virtue. His war with his wife stemmed from his bondage to his mother. The more we explored his erotic arousal with his mother's shoes without shame or contempt, the more he came to understand the meaning of his desire. The more he blessed the holy desire underneath the broken lust, the more he allowed God's delight to expose all that was within that was contrary to love and then allow the Spirit to hover over his sexual chaos and shape it into the beauty of creation.

The Woman's Pursuit (1:2–4)

THE WOMAN
Let him kiss me with the kisses of his mouth,
  for your love is better than wine.
How wonderful is the scent of your oils;
  your name is poured out oil.
Therefore, the young women love you.

Draw me out after you; let's run!
    The king has brought me into his bedroom.

THE WOMEN OF JERUSALEM
We will rejoice and feel happy for you!
    We will praise your love more than wine!

THE WOMAN
They rightly love you!

In the first poem of the Song, the woman speaks of her desire for the man. Note that the woman, not the man, initiates the pursuit of relationship, belying the stereotype found in some religious communities that women need to be passive in relationships, waiting for the man to pursue. Even more, it challenges the notion that a woman is less sexual than a man.

Many assume that a man is more sexual than a woman. Who set this presumptive standard that a woman is not as sexual as a man? A woman is just as sexual as a man, though not in the same way. It appears that God has made male and female to be sufficiently similar in that both desire arousal, pleasure, orgasm, and the intimacy of union, but they are different enough to demand that each submit to a body that is deeply unlike their own in order for both to attain joy.

It is irrefutable that men and women take different paths regarding frequency, intensity, or basis of arousal. Men, it appears, are aroused more by sight. Women relate sexual desire to the quality of the relationship. Many men could have sex soon after a fight; most women would find that too close to the raw emotion of conflict. On the other hand, a woman is more aroused by a man's reputation and social standing. A man is more apt to say he is aroused by a woman whose body fits his image of what is sexy.[7] The differences are both biological and cultural. In every culture men and women are aroused by different sets of criteria, and the criteria change in nearly every age.

The opening line sounds redundant to modern ears: "Let him kiss me with the kisses of his mouth." What other kinds of kisses are there? Perhaps there were other gestures of intimacy in ancient Israel at this time, like nose rubbing or hand holding. But her statement may just be out of exuberance and brings attention to the body parts that come together in the kiss. The Song is sensuous throughout in the sense that lovemaking involves all the senses, but in this poem it begins with the intimate touch of the lips.

She then exclaims that the man's love is better than wine. The Hebrew word translated here as "love" emphasizes the physical aspects of intimacy, not the emotion, although emotion is surely involved. What does wine have to do with physical intimacy? If one has experienced drinking a glass or two, the connection is obvious. Wine is a sensuous liquid, leaving a strong aftertaste on the tongue. Even more to the point, wine makes one lightheaded, just like the kisses of one's beloved. Well, maybe not "just like" kisses, since the woman announces that her man's kisses are even headier than drinking wine.

One reason some Christians today fear drinking wine and (if they are honest) fear the passions of sex is because one becomes lightheaded and loses control. And in fact, sex involves all portions of the brain. There are at least three separable yet profoundly intersecting portions of the brain: reptilian, limbic, and cortical. The reptilian portion regulates autonomic and nonconscious parts of our brain, including our sexual drive. The limbic structure is considered the framework for emotions and the foundation of our pleasure-seeking and pain-fleeing urges. This portion of the brain is more wired to our past experiences that unconsciously shape our inclinations, desires, and fears than to any other part of our brain. And finally, the cortical portion of the brain is involved in story, choice, regulation of desire and affect, and what we normally call thinking.[8]

Our sexuality involves all three parts of our brain, not one alone. One portion of our brain can be at odds with another. We may know that a sexual fantasy or our desire for a specific sexual partner is wrong. We may work hard to stop it, but it simply won't go away. In fact, the more effort we put into derailing the urge, often the stronger it gets. In large measure, it is because we have attempted to tackle a neuropsychological issue that involves cortical, limbic, and reptilian components of our brain with the assumption that if we change our "thinking" our struggle will be resolved. Our sexuality must be engaged at all three levels. The problem is that sexual desire and arousal lessens our higher executive functions (cortical) even as it intensifies our emotional awareness. Simply saying "Use your head" is not as useful in the process of arousal as it is when one is sexually sober.

For many, the loss of optimal cortical control makes sex suspect, if not outright undesirable. Sex is like wine in more ways than one. Both lessen the effect of thought and intensify our capacity to feel. We get "high" with sex and are unable to escape its intoxication.[9] Whether the high is from sex, wine, or drugs, the experience of craving can always be intensified with greater imagery and fantasy. No wonder many shut down sexuality when it appears to be removing our capacity for rational, fully aware, and utterly free choice. But while it is true that we are under the influence of limbic processes through desire and arousal, it is not as if our cortical capacity is gone; it is simply altered, and emotions are in ascendancy. For some people who have been taught not to trust their emotions but to be constantly vigilant and to trust reason instead, it seems unwise to diminish our more rational cortical powers.

However, it is unwise not to bless the way God has made us. In reality one should completely trust neither reason nor emotions; both are affected by sin. But neither our emotions nor our reason are completely warped by sin. God can bring us enjoyments and benefits of the mind and emotions—and marital sex is one way that God delivers his grace to us.

In the poem, the woman's compliments to the man continue. As we will see throughout the Song, compliments are the precursor to intimacy. Compliments need to be honest and not insincere flattery; they need to be authentic in the sense that they are deeply felt. Compliments are necessary to generate the trust that will allow one's beloved to expose himself or herself—not only physically but also emotionally, spiritually, psychologically.

Among the compliments the woman offers is her delight in his scent—her sense of smell thrills at his presence. The "scent of his oils" refers to what today we would call his cologne. A good smell encourages approach and touch. It arouses and invites intimacy. But the thought of his smell leads to another, perhaps more profound, appreciation of the man. His "name" is like poured out oil, oil whose sweet odor permeates a room. "Name" in Hebrew means more than one's moniker. In a context like this one it signifies reputation. She is attracted not only by what he can do to her senses but by his reputation. She respects him, and this respect leads her to want to be close to him.

She then reveals that she knows that she is not the only one who desires him. There are others as well, but she is not surprised that the other women also love him. They confirm her assessment, but she has won his attention. Again, she expresses her desire by wanting him to run away with her, and she excitedly proclaims that the king has brought her into his bedroom.

He is called the king; in other parts of the Song he will be called a shepherd. The Song is a poem, though, and not a historical text. We should not make the mistake of thinking that this king is Solomon. He is king of her heart, not of a nation, and he has brought her into his bedroom. Thus, discreetly, the woman tells us that her desire is consummated in intimate embrace with the man.

The chorus, later identified as the daughters of Jerusalem, affirms the glory and goodness of the couple's relationship. They function here as cheerleaders of the relationship and encourage the man and woman to enjoy their union. Repeating the sentiment of the woman, the couple's love deserves even more praise than wine, which deserves much praise for gladdening the hearts of people (Ps. 104:15). And the woman, not threatened by the attraction of the other women for her man, responds by acknowledging the appropriateness of their affection for him.

Sex intensifies the danger inherent in all relationships. It creates a narrow, at times razor-thin line, between what is holy and lovely and what is profane and ugly. The women adore her man, and this intensifies her desire for him. But this is only a step away from the jealousy that might be felt over their attention. He neither indulges their attention nor turns away from his beloved, yet his erotic presence is palpable and provokes sexual desire in the chorus. Our sexuality, though meant to be intrinsically private, is also part of the public poetic imagination and conversation.

I Will Give You My Love (7:11–13)

THE WOMAN
Come, my love.
Let's go out to the field,
let's spend the night in the villages.

48

Let's go early to the vineyards;
　　let's see if the vine has budded,
　　the bud has opened,
　　the pomegranates have bloomed.
There I will give my love to you!
The mandrakes give forth their scent,
　　and on our entrance is every precious gift.
The new as well as the old,
　　I have treasured up for you, my love.

In this short poem, a love monologue, the woman again speaks her desire for intimacy with the man. She beckons him to go to the countryside with her. In the logic of the love poetry of the Song, the countryside with its vineyards, orchards, and gardens is the place of lovemaking, in contrast to city settings, which are hostile to intimacy (5:2–7). After all, while the city teems with people, the countryside suggests the privacy that encourages intimacy. Thus, her desire to go with him to the countryside is an invitation to bliss.

She entices him to investigate the new growth of the vineyards. From her description one can almost smell the sweet aroma of the vines. But it is of special significance that she wonders whether the vine has budded, the bud has opened, the pomegranates have bloomed. In other words, it is not just any time in the garden—it is the springtime. In antiquity as well as today, the springtime resonates with love. After the winter, it is the time to take clothes off, to enjoy the warm wind on the body, to bask in the sunlight. Spring is the time of fertility, growth, new life, and joy. The sights and smells of a springtime vineyard make for a pleasant fantasy setting for romance.

The woman's ultimate desire is no secret. In a climactic statement, she announces, "There I will give my love to you!" using a Hebrew word for love again that foregrounds the physical rather than the emotional nature of love. Though motivated by love and not lust, she thus asserts her desire to grant the gift of sexual pleasure to the man.

She continues to evoke an erotic setting, now mentioning mandrakes that give forth their smell. The specific mention of the mandrake is not arbitrary in this expression of desire. The mandrake was known in antiquity as a plant that could heighten desire and the pleasures of touch—in other words, an aphrodisiac (see Gen. 30:14–16). Indeed, the Hebrew name of the plant (*duda'im*) is very close in spelling and pronunciation to a common word for love or lover in the Hebrew of the Song of Songs (*dwd*).

The use of aphrodisiacs as a means to generate or intensify sexual desire is blessed. We know that the fruit of a mandrake plant can be used with other plants as a sedative and that its roots are poisonous, capable of causing death. Did it truly work as an aphrodisiac? We simply don't know. The most widely used and debated aphrodisiac used today is dark chocolate. There is no proof that it has the capacity to arouse, but it unquestionably raises dopamine, the biochemical associated with pleasure. Viagra, though not considered an aphrodisiac, is in fact a drug that changes the capacity for an erection, and therefore is associated with the anticipation of arousal. As we know from the power of the placebo effect, many times it is our capacity to imagine the effects of good that alter our brain's basic biochemistry. The point is that sex is as much, if not more, a matter of the brain as it is a matter of one's primary or secondary sexual organs. And God blesses what arouses us when the erotic stimulation violates neither the love of God nor the love of others.

As the poem unfolds, the woman has treasures to give her man as they enter their vineyard bedroom. They are described rather generally as "new" things as well as "old," which suggests the origins of the modern practice of giving a bride "something old, something new." But here it is an ancient Hebrew way of saying that she will give him everything that is near and dear to her, especially her own self, body and soul.

An Invitation to a Tryst (1:7–8)

THE WOMAN
Tell me, one whom I love, where will you graze?
    Where will you make your flocks lie down at noon?
Why should I be like a veiled woman
    around the flocks of your companions?

THE MAN
If you do not know, most beautiful of women,
    follow the tracks of the sheep,
    and feed your young goats
    by the dwellings of the shepherds.

This brief poem is a playful dialogue between the man and the woman. Notice that yet again she initiates the verbal foreplay that provokes him to respond in this teasing interchange. She addresses him as a shepherd, though in the first poem (1:2–4) she calls him her king. Perhaps it is appropriate to give a reminder that we are dealing not with an actual person but with love poetry that can apply to many. The king and the shepherd are not two different individuals, nor is the king called a shepherd. These roles are just part of the poetic fantasy conjured up by the poet. By speaking of the man as a shepherd, a country setting is immediately evoked in the imagination, and as we observed in the preceding poem, the countryside is the place of privacy and intimacy in distinction from the city.

That said, to be alone the woman must navigate the presence of other shepherds in order to come, unnoticed, into the privacy of her beloved's tent. Those with prosaic minds might ask the question, If they are married (see the introduction above), then why do they care who sees her coming out to him? In the first place, ancient societies do not operate like modern ones, but even today if a wife went to a husband's place of work to initiate sex, it would probably be a bit awkward for his colleagues. Further, we note elsewhere in the Song that public displays of affection, even a kiss (8:1–4), were considered unseemly in ancient Israel, at least at the time this poem was written.

Cultural mores obviously play a huge role in determining what is arousing and what is considered scandalous or aberrant. In the West an uncovered female breast is considered erotic while in parts of Africa an exposed breast would not turn a head. In the same way, two men holding hands or walking arm in arm in Europe would not be interpreted the same as in the United States. It is naive to think that culture doesn't play a profound role in sexuality. Most peoples' stance toward cultural norms has usually been to both abide by and test, if not break, the boundaries. Often boundaries attempt to protect and conserve; but arousal is to some degree related to the desire to risk, to push beyond what some consider safe. It is a strange linkage: we need safety to be able to relax, but too much rest moves us in the direction of boredom. We need danger to experience a heightening of arousal, but not so much that it generates shame and a flooding of fear. Like every other dimension of sexuality, culture can create paradox.[10]

She wants to meet him at noon, so she asks him where he will take his sheep to graze. If she meets him at noon, she has to negotiate the complications of running into other shepherds. It is a risk that chances cultural boundary violations. She wants to know because she does not want to go tent to tent searching for him. After all, that would make her look as if she is a "veiled woman." Once again, modern readers need help to understand the allusion. A "veiled woman" going tent to tent would be a prostitute. She is going to his tent for sex, but she is not asking for money. She is not of course a prostitute, but she puts it this way to try to elicit an answer from him.

He answers her, but only indirectly in order to tease and arouse her. The poem reads like a playful, sensual game of hide and seek. He says that she should act like a shepherd herself, but follow along behind. She should lead her goats along the path left earlier by his flock. That will bring her to him under the guise of a shepherd. The implicit message is that they will successfully achieve the privacy they both want in order to consummate their love and the arousal of breaking the "paradigm" of what is expected in "appropriate" sexual activity between a husband and wife.

The Invitation (4:8–9)

THE MAN
With me from Lebanon, my bride;
with me, from Lebanon, come!
Come down from the top of Amana;
from the top of Senir and Hermon,
from the dens of lions,
from the heights of leopards.
You drive me crazy, my sister, my bride!
You drive me crazy
with one glance of your eyes,
with one jewel from your necklace.

While this short poem may actually be part of a larger poem that we will treat in chapter 7, we highlight it here because it testifies to the man's desire. The previous three poems have all spoken to the woman's yearning for intimacy, so it is important to see evidence of the man's hopes as well. Again, as mentioned earlier, the fact that there are three poems that speak to the woman's desire and only one for the man throws suspicion on the still-common view that women should be passive in relationship, waiting for a man to initiate and guide. Not only these but other poems that we will consider later in the book will show the woman active, even aggressive, in pursuit of love.

But neither is the man passive. His words are a powerfully charged invitation to enter his protective embrace. He wants her to be "with him." We must again remember that this is poetry and that the woman is not literally living in a den of wild animals on some mountain in Lebanon.[11] The mountains of Lebanon are a distant place, way up north. Three mountains are mentioned, all well known in antiquity, but best known today is snow-capped Hermon, which stands near the present-day border of Israel and Lebanon. But her mountain dwelling represents not only distance but also danger. It is the place of predator animals, of lions and leopards. Is she in danger or does she inhabit a world of danger? The poem is so nuanced we are left to wonder. He seems to be saying that she is a woman comfortable in danger, and yet he wants the distance between them to evaporate. There is something about her and her beauty that is wild and cannot be tamed. It is a beauty that excites him and invites him to surrender to the ecstasy her beauty elicits. It is perhaps equivalent to saying to your partner, "You look hot!" Her sexuality is wild yet distant; he wants her close and wildly alive.[12]

In verse 9, he can hardly control himself when he says to her, "You drive me crazy." Of course, this is a translation of the Hebrew that uses a contemporary idiom. The Hebrew verb is rare and is formed from the Hebrew noun for "heart," in a form that expresses a highly emotional state. The word refers to the man's excited emotional state as he thinks of the woman. In its ancient Near Eastern context, though, it may have additional resonance. Scholars refer to the use of "heart" in Mesopotamian literature and in particular sexual potency rituals called "rising of the heart" texts in which what is rising is more than the emotions.[13]

And it does not take much from the woman to get his heart racing. Just one glance of her eyes, just one jewel of her necklace. Of course, he wants all of her! That is not the point. But even a hint of her overwhelms him. Desire is flooding his senses with anticipation, orienting him to her and to nothing else.

It is important to say something about the terms of endearment by which he addresses her. The first needs little explanation. She is his "bride." Perhaps this song is one sung on the marriage day, perhaps long after the wedding, but in any case, this epithet squarely plants the poem in a marriage context (see the introduction for the connection between the Song and marriage). It is, however, the second title that throws modern readers off. He calls her his sister. It needs to be understood that, as ancient Egyptian love poems confirm, she is not his literal sister. In the post-Moses period, a marriage between a brother and a sister would have been considered incest, as it is today (Lev. 18:9; 20:17). Perhaps the New Living Translation has taken the best approach in capturing the ancient intent for a modern reader when it translates the literal but misleading "sister" as "my treasure." She is indeed his coveted bride and treasure.

Summary

Desire is the water of the soul. Its absence spells the loss of the lush green and verdant fruit of love. Without desire the soul becomes a desert and the body loses its vitality. In fact, a body without desire not only sags and is sapped of energy but in due season succumbs to despair, if not death. But desire can also be a rushing torrent ripping down trees and flooding a quiet plain. The goal is a perfect amount that generates life but doesn't overwhelm. We may alternately or simultaneously adore or abhor desire; but in either case, desire moves the body and heart to pursue the dream—or is it best to say, the desire embedded in story? We need to learn to listen to what our desires reveal about the story that is actually moving us forward toward sexual consummation. We don't desire or fantasize about the actual seconds of orgasm. It is the yearning to be connected and caught up in a process that leads to ecstasy that moves us.

We are desire-fueled beings. We can do nothing without desire, and desire fills our acts, whether consciously or not. Many of our sexual fantasies and behaviors are fueled by desires that are profoundly deeper than an orgasm or even love. It is often this unaddressed realm of meaning that stymies most movement toward holiness. We simply fail to understand what is really moving us.

Does a man look at pornography just for the arousal and prompt to masturbate? Is his struggle that he is simply too sexual and is focusing on the wrong person? Or is it possible his desire is to be chosen by and to magnetically draw a woman of such beauty that she would do anything for his delight? The desire to look at pornography is belittling to both the woman and the man; the desire to be captured by delight, however, is one of the most lovely and holy desires of our heart.

The poets of intimate sexual desire draw us to the whimsical hunger for danger and play, privacy and boldness. Holy sexual desire is a sharp two-edged sword that cuts on one side against wantonness and crudity and on the other against dutifulness or prudery. To be more direct, sexual desire must combine a commitment to honor and care as well as playful flirtation, intense arousal, and carefree pleasure.

Desire traps us and reveals that we seldom honor desire and sensuality as holy because of the inherent tensions that arise

> The desire to be captured by delight is one of the most lovely and holy desires of our heart.

from our impure hearts. But the nature of desire is that it not only moves the body, but it awakens the heart to something unfathomably deeper than mere physical pleasure. It calls the heart in the midst of one of the most immanent experiences of life—sex—to desire something no less wild, holy, and beautiful: the transcendent delight of God.

5

After the
Bible Study on Desire

Okay, Mr. (or is it Ms.?) Diary—ready for a wild ride? I got into Agnes, started her up, and felt both the metal doors and my sides involuntarily shake. My body waited until I got into the car to break into a sweat. I had to get away from Jon's house as fast as I could, pulling over after a few blocks. I got out and began to walk the well-manicured streets of their suburb.

I know suburbs. I grew up in the privileged starter palaces of the upper middle class; I flirted with friends who knew the august heights of wealth. This is not a new world to me, but as I walked, it all felt too obvious—the richer you are, the farther you can live from your neighbors.

And the farther away, the less they can see or feel the sweat running down your face or your sides shaking. I thought about the time I was in Mumbai. Every moment the smell of the ever-present decaying humanity scoured me with the paradox of life teeming around the dying and dead. Here in this "burb" there is no death, only the illusion of life through the flickering televisions hidden seductively behind the see-through curtains. I peered into a few homes. I didn't see anyone clearly, but I did see an occasional ghost or shadow pass from one room to another, or a light flicker on or off.

The ding of a cell phone message startled me awake; I am thankful, or I might have stood looking into the house until I was arrested. My sweat had cooled and I was beginning to regain my composure until I said the words out loud. "I told the group I was aroused by older women."

Prior to that moment the whole group time had felt like I was stuck in the molasses of an eighth-grade dance. I remember trying to make my way from the table that held the one thing acceptable to focus on—cookies and powdered lemonade from a large yellow cylindrical container—past the horde of giggling girls to ask Nancy Metcalf to dance. I don't recall how I made the decision to ask; I just moved. As I passed the gaggle I heard someone snicker and others whisper in loud, theatrical voices, and I knew they were watching me climb the steep slope to where Nancy was sitting. She saw me coming and likely saw the craven terror in my eyes, or perhaps the light pulsing off the glinting grease of my oily face. The two new pimples on the left side of my nose were like cherry tomatoes in an Italian salad. Before I could reach her, she rose and walked away rapidly to find someone to save her from the humiliation of being asked by Malcolm to dance.

It was as if I reached out into thin air and tried to embrace a phantom dream that I didn't have the courage to desire or pursue prior to that moment. I just moved toward her in a fog of jumbled, broken intentions. I just moved. At the moment, with the whole thing dissolved in my memory, I found myself in the group saying that I seldom feel aroused by women my age or younger. I feel sexually far more at ease with seasoned sexual confidantes whose skin is not as soft or taut, but whose hands make the first move.

What possessed me to say that out loud? They were silent. I was so relieved when Lois said, "That's just not right. Is that what we are to do in this group? To divulge our dark, ugly secrets?"

The patina of disgust was thick as a whore's mascara. The group at first had been silent and now the noise of their discomfort was thick and stuck in their throats. But I felt immense relief. Lois was my savior, my erotic doppelganger—as ugly as I felt inside, she acted out against me and it felt heavenly.

Then, in the center of the awkward silence, Jon said, "Thank you, Malcolm, for sharing. And Lois, you are naming something so important for us all that we need to stop and make sure we progress forward slowly and well. First, there needs to be a commitment not to judge anyone's sexual desires or behavior, no matter how clearly it offends you, scares you, or how much it seems to violate what we know about the Bible."

But Lois was on a roll. "I know you are talking directly to me because what he shared obviously provokes me. Maybe it's not wrong, but it at least seems weird he is aroused by women his mother's age. Look, I have had all the sexual weirdness I ever need to hear about after living with my husband for twelve years. I really don't know if I should be here."

Then the chatter—rapid-fire female voices with the lilt of maternal counsel, drowning out the tension with the milk of compassion.

"Lois, it is okay to question if this is the right group and time for you—you've been terribly hurt. Thank you for your honesty."

I don't recall what brought about the shift but all eyes were off me and on Lois. She leaned back and unfolded her arms.

"Malcolm, I am aware that my words are harsh. I wish I could apologize, but it wouldn't even be close to honest. I do judge you, and even if I shouldn't, I don't know how to do any better at the moment other than to say what I've said."

Before I could tell her that was fine with me, Amihan said, "I am so grateful for both of you. Malcolm, your honesty is refreshing. I, too, have sexual desires I assumed I would never, and I mean never, ever be able to talk about. Just to be able to say to you all that I have sexual desire that feels more than wrong is a relief. And dear Lois, I am so grateful for your outburst. I don't know if Jon was talking directly to you, but I know he is talking straight to me. I am so freaked out at the thought that others are sexual, live in their own private sexual realm, and do sexual things behind closed doors, that it just feels prudish to admit it. It is easier for me to judge everyone else. You both have given me permission to struggle sexually and to admit how judgmental I am."

Amihan looked like she was about to pass the baton to the next fool who wanted to jump into the fray, but then she sat forward and spoke again.

"I was really afraid that tonight was going to be a litany of confessions that the men struggle with pornography and the women struggle to want sex more. And I'm sure most of the men struggle with pornography and most of the women think they don't want sex enough, but I struggle with pornography and I want sex too much. I am a virgin and I am chaste, but I am a mess. In fact, the reason I am a virgin has little to do with my morality and the rightness of waiting for the man of my dreams in marriage, as much as it does with my fear of a thousand other things that I don't understand and a few dozen that I do."

Even a few hours later trying to remember all that I heard is nearly impossible. The conversation flowed on, but I think it will be easier for me to write out what I remember each person said rather than figure out how it was all woven together.

Jon was the first to go as we began to share about desire. He said he had access at an early age to troves of pornography. What lingers for him is the idea that a woman would be easy—easy to attract, easy to please, and easy to bring to orgasm. Life and his wife, Celeste, have exposed that illusion; yet, he finds himself easily drawn back to the fantasy, and then irritated at Celeste for not being what his dreams tell him she should be.

I wasn't stunned by what he said—I've heard the complaints before. But where Jon has found women (specifically Celeste) difficult in these ways sexually, I've found women to be easy. The other men, even the women, seem to take it as the gospel truth that men find women difficult to understand and to cope with. He set the stage by asking us to name what we bring to our sexuality that has informed our desire and shaped it. I was especially glad that he said we didn't need to share any particulars of our current sexual struggle or sin. Thank God. We can wander this terrain like abstractions.

What blew me away was the honesty of Celeste. She admitted she was not an easy partner, nor had a lot of interest in sex. She said she grew up in a world that felt like as long as she was on the beach, life was sunny and safe; but the moment she stepped into the water, the music from *Jaws* began to play. Sex was death, unless you had the magic buffer called marriage to whisk you away from the sharks. All one had to do was wait. Freeze dry desire and with the first hot water it came back to life like a time-elapsed video that condenses ten years into two minutes. Sex is good, beautiful—or so she was told in her conservative church; but it always felt too dangerous to desire.

Celeste's warmth soon dissipated, a shadow came over her face. "I won't go into details, but the prime way I got aroused as an adolescent was to fantasize being taken and hurt by a man who I knew wanted to do nothing but use me."

I wanted to scream at them both—sex can be as easy as your freedom not to care. If you care, you'll be hurt—or at least confused. If you just go with nothing more than the rhythm of the deed, then you can enjoy it for what it is and not worry about what it isn't. Be in the moment, forget the past, postpone the future, and then sex is not only the best form of denial but is the best substitute for reality that only an illusion can offer. I know enough to know that sounds too godless, but it still seems true.

Eventually Marty and Jill took the stage. It felt like a well-orchestrated burlesque with just enough sincerity to confess that neither had inhaled. Marty admitted on both of their behalfs that they had each been unfaithful to their first spouse by having an affair with each other that ended their marriages. I kept noticing Marty's quicksilver hair. His hair moved like strands of grey snakes. His hair seemed alive and more interesting than its owner. Marty was attractive but somewhat witless. He was too impressed with himself to be seductive, but he was obviously wealthy and knew how to charm. He knew, at least, how to charm a younger woman.

I couldn't believe he told us her story. He went on to tell us that Jill had been sexually abused by her father and had been addicted to drugs and hung out with an East Coast band for a couple of years. Jill didn't flinch. Obviously her story was not her own.

Jill was younger, but her face showed the grooves of a lot of late nights, barbiturates, and bad music. Most of her creases were filled by too much foundation, giving her face a stale brown rigidity. It was impossible to look at her without wanting to run my hands down her face and tell her it was okay; to let her tears wash away the false tint. You could tell there was still a pale presence that was breathing below the surface, but it was laboring to fill her lungs. I tried not to stare at her, and soon thereafter I made my confession.

I think it happened soon after I tried in my mind to ask Nancy to dance in eighth grade. She fled to the safety of the gaggle that was giggling at my presumption. I should have known that I was not in her stratum. I stood mouth agape, eyes wide and bewildered, in the place where she had just been sitting. I must have stood there for two or three minutes. I felt a hand on my arm. It was my English teacher, Mrs. Gunnerson. She smiled and the sun poured out from her eyes. I felt her warmth and she laughed, "Malcolm, Malcolm—just as I told you in class, not all books are worth reading." I looked at her with even greater bewilderment. "C'mon, Malcolm, help me bring in a load of cookies and brownies from the kitchen."

I followed her. I remembered looking at her high heels and tapered jeans. When we got to the kitchen she brushed my arm again, this time moving her hand up and down slowly and deliberately. I don't recall what she was saying. I just knew I wanted to run. I saw my dulled reflection in the metal countertop and didn't recognize my face. I don't remember much else other than she held me close and kissed me, making me feel as if I didn't know how to breathe.

I was erect. I felt humiliated at its protruding angle, and as suddenly Mrs. Gunnerson turned and walked back to the dance with a tray of cookies. I wanted her; I wanted to be like water and evaporate. Now the images pass by so quickly that I don't know if it is a dream or a furtive memory. Then the words came out of my mouth, all of a sudden saying to the group, "I am more aroused by older women than girls my age."

I don't know why I turned to see Celeste's face first. She didn't look dismayed or flirtatious. Her face was quiet and sad. It was easier to look away and see the roiling disgust in Lois's eyes. I knew she was about to skewer me, and I felt a calm, expectant anticipation in the bloodletting. I knew I could submit to her cruelty and feel the emancipation from desire that was swelling in me.

Desire. What am I to learn from the Bible discussion tonight? I don't recall much of what was said about the Song. Jon and Celeste talked about how desire reflects what God breathed into our hearts and something about how evil, the devil, or someone works to twist it and use it to torture. I tried to look interested, but as much as this is a Bible study, it felt more like a therapy group. But a few more things stuck with me.

The Song glories in the goodness of a woman's desire—not exactly my experience. And the passage that says "his name is like poured out oil" made me feel nauseous. What is my name? What is my reputation among women? All I know is my reputation was not fragrant; it reeked of the heat of body fluids, sweat, and incense. I wanted to bathe to cover the odor. I can arouse a woman without being quick to arousal; I can be seduced and perform at the top of my game, and still make it clear I am an aloof, albeit attentive servant.

My reputation—I am good at sex without caring. And it is that capacity to not care and her hope that she can bring light to the dark side of my moon that makes me so desirable and, in the long run, detestable. I bring pleasure and awaken her desire for power; then I let myself be swallowed without being consumed. It's all so vulgar.

Sweetness. I walk away from the desires of the Songstress feeling sick. What is wrong with me? I feel like I am sinking in quicksand and if I attempt to move I sink deeper. If I remain impassive I will sink as surely, only at a slower rate. In either case, I want and I don't want. I want my partner playful, innocent. I suppose that is where I am stuck. Innocence. It is not real; it was never true. But then why do I crave to be touched, to touch and have it be truly good and unfettered, given what sloshes inside me?

Maybe all I can take away from tonight is that someone, somewhere knew sweet and sensual holiness—even if only in an ancient poem. If not, then it is fiction—or what my college psych professors would call an infantile illusion. If it is nothing more than an illusion, then it is certainly a better one than the whimsical hope that another sexual moment will free me.

I think I am going to have to take Pascal's bet. If I say there is nothing holy and true, then I take that position by faith. If I operate on the hope that it is possible to be sexual and innocent, I can only do so equally by faith. In either case, I have to operate on the basis of faith. It is a bet. I'm going to double down on that bet.

6

Before the
Bible Study on Beauty

After the group I had a long talk with—drum roll—Lois. We had parked near each other and we both walked to our cars like we were lost in a snowstorm. We couldn't quite look at each other, and when we finally did, both of us were suffused in a whiteout. I hazily remember her words.

"Malcolm—your confession triggered me and disgusted me. I am sorry." It was quick and hit me like a hammer.

"No worries, Lois. No problemo."

"No, don't flick me off like a fly. If that is all my apology is worth to you then I really am a fool."

Her last word was said with a quiet, exhaling sadness. It made me stop and for a moment look through the swirling flakes to see her eyes. She wasn't disgusted; she wasn't just ticked. She was bold, fragile. I couldn't help but stare. She turned away and the whiteout returned for us both, but I knew I didn't want to remain out in the cold. I simply didn't know what else to say. All I could say to her was "Okay."

Later I called Jon and had a beer with him at the Harbor Pub. Because of the ruckus around us, he had to lean into the middle of the table to hear me.

We were almost yelling at each other. I rolled the story of the teacher over to him as casually as sliding over the guacamole. I could see his eyes glisten, heard his voice waver, "Malcolm, what you just described is sexual abuse." I took his words in without blinking. I am not a particularly angry man, but I wanted to laugh in his face after blinding him with a Belgian ale. I shrugged. He said it again. This time I looked out the window to the water below. The masts of the sailboats beat out a metronome tick tock and waited for time to stop. It didn't.

Jon reminded me that for the next group meeting I was supposed to think about what I found beautiful. I felt so tired I could barely wave him off as we parted in the parking lot.

I do have one memory that makes me think of something beautiful.

I was supposed to meet a friend at a restaurant; I was riding my bike all decked out in my commuting rain gear, sporting my flashing red light on the rear and my bright, epilepsy-provoking strobe on the front. I saw my friend talking with someone at a light and rode by her and stopped a block away. I got off and bolted my horse to the bike rack and then sat on a bench next to a women's crisis care clinic while I waited for her to pass.

I prepared the moment like a seven-course feast. I knew the second she passed to look in her face and watch her turn away from the rude male casting a "gaze" directly in her eyes; I knew she would look, see my eyes, avert her face with irritation bordering on disdain, then realize who I was, and turn back with both surprise and the slightest hint of shame. It was a piece of performance art.

She cried out, "Malcolm, you."

I felt my whole body tingle with delight. It worked. The silly little plan worked and everything I had hoped came out just as I anticipated. And this is my encounter with something beautiful? I don't deny I am still a boy-man, a cowboy, but my plan worked. If she hadn't turned away with embarrassment and irritation, it would have all been ruined. If she hadn't turned back with slight indignity and then recognition and laughter, it would have all been lost. Such a passing, ephemeral moment, like building an elaborate sand castle whose ramparts will momentarily melt before the foam. It was all innocent play—anticipation and fulfillment, a sweet game whose parts harmonized in laughter. I wish it made more sense. All I know is the plan went better than I imagined. I knew I wanted to surprise her, but what I really wanted I had not named. I simply wanted her to laugh with me, to play with me without any sexual plot or overtones.

We laughed for longer than it was worth, but I found that even at the end of the day I still relished those moments more than making $15K after selling a used truck to a volunteer fire department in Deadwood, South Dakota.

To prepare us to think about beauty in our next session, Jon said, "Beauty takes our breath away and gives us back something that fills our lungs with fresh, life-giving air." Sounded to me like good pot, but thankfully I kept my mouth shut. What intrigued me, however, was his claim that beauty is profoundly elusive. It's hard to define, he said, and we have to keep our eyes open to what we consider beautiful and to how it captures and transforms us. I made it my goal to be ready for beauty. Lo and behold, beauty arrived—why did I find that moment so beautiful?

I keep thinking the plan worked, but it was more than a successful completion of a task. I knew her well enough to know she would be mildly offended at someone staring directly into her eyes, and then I knew her well enough to know that when she recognized me she would be undone. I thought she might smack me, but instead it was the sound of her voice, "Malcolm"—with a rise on the first syllable. *Malcolm. Bad* boy.

It just delighted me to anticipate and predict, plan and then execute, all for a laugh. We laughed over something that just didn't matter, and it felt freeing to connect with someone and know in that moment it was all that was needed—nothing more was being asked of me, nor did I want more. It was enough. The moment was enough, and yet it was like riding a wave that didn't end through our entire breakfast.

I felt sick when she ended up taking a call and then rushing off to meet her boyfriend. I didn't want her to leave and, far more, I didn't want the perfection of the moment to end. I knew the little scare would be good for a laugh and maybe a story when we were together with other friends, but once she left the table, I knew the beautiful moment was done. There, I said it: it was beautiful.

So what do I consider to be signs of the beautiful? When it comes to beauty, I know I am mesmerized, literally transfixed by Chagall. I've read enough about his life that I think he was a narcissistic toad, especially to his son. But somehow I forget about him and lose myself in the riot of color and Russian fabulist Jewish mysticism. I know I am taken by Gerard Manley Hopkins and Flannery O'Connor.

I'm listening to Van Morrison as I pen these silly thoughts. I know. I can't escape the fact that my father loves Chagall and Van Morrison. Beauty, whatever it is, was on the wall, read, and sung before I knew about paintings, poems, or songs. And so am I little more than the tastes and preferences of someone else?

My father was a sensuous man. He loved women, fine scotch, Romeo y Julieta cigars—only Cubans, of course. He was busy, gone, traveling. When he was home, he immersed himself in what gave his weary body rest: beauty. He sucked from the marrow of beauty like a ravenous wolf. And he tossed a few scraps to his son, and I too devoured them, but only after I dragged them far from his presence. I don't know if I was afraid he would notice and take them back, or worse—afraid that he would notice and feel some delight that I was eating from his spoil.

I could never show him that I was like him. He ate with abandon, and I hoard my food. Grease covered his face, and his laugh was brazen; I am called delicate, and I don't laugh as much as I would like. But I share, or stole, my father's sense of what is beautiful, even if I am not barrel-chested, bold, and overtly sexual in the conquering-Roman style.

So I know what I like, but I don't know why I find anything or anyone beautiful. I am not sure it is worth the time I have already spent, but I do find myself troubled by what I desire, what I find beautiful.

I got an email from Lois. She wrote:

Malcolm, we didnt finish the conversation and we dont need to, but it has become clearer to me that for all your suave assurance, you are just scared. You brush me and others off like lint. Thats what I felt like when you just walked away to your car. But then sometime later i realized i dont brush anyone off like lint. I slam them like a door. I just want you to know i didnt always slam doors. I used to be terrified to darken any door — it always meant walking into a room and i didnt know what was going to be required — i still dont but when my marriage came to a bad spot i knew i was either going to let him make fun of me and make me small or i was going to need to really grow up and go through whatever doors i had to walk through. I m not giving you advice, but then again i probably am. all i know is i am not lint nor are you a door to be slammed. and i am still sorry for what i said even though it still grosses me out. Lois

It's the first time I have been within ten miles of tears for a long, long time. Troubling, weird woman.

7

The Intrigue of Beauty

Beauty, like air, is available to all, yet so fleeting. It takes but a moment for a sun in its fiery blaze to sink into the ocean. It is said that a person's beauty fades with age. Yet beauty bears a weight that can't be ignored. But what is often preferred to true beauty is an airbrushed version. It seems we prefer the unreal to the real and the profane to the holy.

Catulle Mendès, a French poet in the time of Napoleon III, is said to have been walking one evening in Paris when he noticed groups of men, young and old, well and poorly dressed, all enjoying coin peep shows of nude or partially nude women from a row of slot machines. However, there was one machine that all the men seemed to avoid. In his curiosity he dropped in his penny and found it was a picture of the sculpture of the Venus de Medici. He surmised their lack of excitement about her was because she was beautiful. She was no less feminine or naked than the pictures the men were enjoying, but her image lacked the vulgarity.[1]

The beauty of the body is difficult to behold and surrender to without making it tolerable by commodifying it or putting it into the category of obscenity. Therefore many have sought to altogether avoid any conversations regarding it, except in the Songs.

The most erotic, striking, and sensuous speeches in the Song are the poems in which the man describes the woman's physical beauty and the woman lingers on the man's appealing appearance. The descriptions begin with either the partner's head or feet and then work down or up to the object of erotic focus. Neither the man nor the woman is a prude; they celebrate every part of their lover's body. That said, these poems are not crude. Rather, they speak in terms of tasteful metaphors that arouse as they both reveal and conceal the person they describe. Such poems intend to inspire married couples today to revel in their spouse's bodily beauty.

From Head to Breasts (4:1–7)

THE MAN
Behold, you are beautiful, my darling!
   Behold you are beautiful,
and your eyes are doves behind your veil.
   Your hair is like a flock of goats streaming from Mount
   Gilead.
Your teeth are like a flock of shorn sheep, coming up from a
   washing.
   Each is paired; not one of them is missing.
Like a scarlet thread are your lips,
   and your mouth is desirable.
Like a slice of pomegranate is your temple
   behind your veil.
Like the tower of David is your neck,
   built in courses.
A thousand shields are hung on it;
   all are bucklers of heroes.
Your two breasts are like two fawns,
   twins of a gazelle,
   grazing among the lilies.
Until the day breaks and the shadows flee,
   I myself will go to the mountain of myrrh
   and to the hills of frankincense.
You are totally beautiful, my darling.
   You have no blemish.

As we will see, this poem is paired to and continues in 4:10–5:1, which we will explore in a moment, but it has its own unity that begins and ends with the man's affirmation of the woman's beauty. Between the opening and the closing, he speaks specifically of her eyes, her hair, her teeth, her lips and mouth, her temple, her neck, and her breasts. And these are words spoken not just for his own imagination or her objectification, but they are words spoken to her.

> These are words spoken not just for his own imagination or her objectification, but they are words spoken to her.

Every age and every culture has its own metaphors for beauty, and the Song's imagery often strikes us as strange, so we will take some time to explain it here. Even without explanation one feels its vibrant sensuality; the language drips with desire.

He starts with her head—specifically, her eyes. The eyes are a window to the soul. No one knows who first said this, but it is interesting that from an early age we are instructed to look people in the eyes when we speak with them. In the Bible, David's beauty is associated with his eyes (1 Sam. 16:12), while the mention of Leah's "weak eyes" (as the Hebrew literally says in Gen. 29:17) contrasts with Rachel's beauty.

The lover is obviously attracted to his beloved's eyes, but in the final analysis the meaning of the metaphor escapes us. How are eyes like doves? *The Dictionary of Biblical Imagery* lists a number of qualities that may be at play here when it refers to "the dove's softness, beauty of feathers and eyes, and affection for the faithfulness of its mate."[2] We are missing a cultural background to this image, but from the context we can be certain that the metaphor is a compliment.

The beauty of her eyes is accentuated by being "behind [her] veil." Perhaps the veil was transparent or it covered everything but her eyes (though he does describe her teeth). Whichever it is, the veil both hides beauty and heightens desire. The glimpse of physical beauty is more evocative than seeing the whole. The view of the part arouses the desire to see the whole.

Next, her hair is compared to a flock of goats streaming down from Mount Gilead. The Song will often use geographical references in its imagery. These are places that would have been well known to the original audience but are opaque to a modern reader. Why Gilead? Perhaps because it is a beautiful place in that part of that world. Gilead refers to the region in the central Transjordan that surrounds the Jabbok River. It was a distant and awe-inspiring place. The goats, black, stream down, giving the impression of lush, flowing hair that captures the man's attention.

Still focused on her face, he next lovingly comments on her teeth. The compliment that "not one of them is missing" strikes a modern audience as bizarre. What woman would feel moved by her lover making a point that she has all her teeth? However, we must remember the ancient context, a time before the development of dental hygiene or even toothpaste, which makes it all the more remarkable that her teeth are as white as a flock of sheep just washed and shorn. The emphasis here, as we will see elsewhere in the poem, is on symmetry (each has its twin).

Verse 3 completes the sensuous description of her face with a look at her lips and her temples. Her lips are like a scarlet ribbon, deep red, perhaps referring to the natural color of her lips or perhaps, since the ancients—like modern women—used cosmetics, referring to the beauty of her lips enhanced by the ancient equivalent of lipstick.[3] As for her temples, they are like pomegranates, another image difficult for us to penetrate, though it likely refers to her pleasing dark complexion.

Moving down from her face, the man compares her neck to the tower of David. The association with David grants this image a sense of power and dignity. Since this verse is the only mention in the Bible of a tower associated with David, we do not know what it looked like. In any case, the comparison is probably not a visual one, but rather a comparison of value. That is, like the tower of David, her neck is dignified and majestic. One scholar suggests that it may be a picture of both "proud reticence and provocative liveliness."[4] This tower has a thousand shields of heroes surrounding it. The custom of hanging ornamental shields on the outer wall of a tower is known from ancient times, and the image likely connects with a necklace that hung around the woman's neck, enhancing her beauty and dignity.

Moving down again on the woman's body, the man now comes to her breasts. Notice again the focus on symmetry. He says not that they are large or small but that they are "twins." Specifically the breasts are twin gazelles that have their heads down grazing in the lilies. What picture does the poet want us to imagine?

In the first place, the gazelle communicates the quality of sleek sensuality, but what of its pose? Often readers imagine the scene as if looking at the gazelles from the front, but that makes no real sense as an image for the woman's breasts. Indeed, rather than the front we should picture the gazelles from the rear. As they graze, their rounded rumps with their nipple-like tails are prominently displayed, inviting comparison with the woman's desirable breasts.

At this point in the poem, the man, overwhelmed by desire, breaks away from his poetic rhapsody about her body. He states his intention to go to the "mountain of myrrh," to the "hills of frankincense," metaphors that can only stand for the woman herself. Myrrh is a fragrant resin, and the mountains of Lebanon are also sweet smelling because of Lebanon's association with the cedar tree, and both refer to the sensual body of the woman. In this way, he describes his desire to be physically intimate with her.

While this statement of desire brings a sense of closure to this particular poem, the poet will pick up where he left off in the next poem we will explore. He will bring us to the ultimate place of his erotic interest, her garden fountain.

Eating in the Garden of Love (4:10–5:1)

THE MAN

How beautiful your love, my sister, my bride!
    How much better your love than wine
and the scent of your oils than spices!
Your lips drip honey, O bride.
    Honey and milk are under your tongue.
    The scent of your garments is like the scent of Lebanon.
You are a locked garden, my sister, my bride.
    You are a locked garden, a sealed fountain.
Your "shoots" are a garden of pomegranates
    with choice fruits,

henna and nard,
    nard and saffron,
calamus and cinnamon,
    with every kind of incense tree,
myrrh and aloes,
    with all the chief spices.
You are a garden fountain,
    a well of living water,
        streaming down from Lebanon.

THE WOMAN
Wake up, north wind,
    and come, south wind!
Blow on my garden
    and let its spices flow forth.
Let my lover come into his garden
    and eat its choice fruit.

THE MAN
I have come into my garden, my sister, my bride.
    I have gathered my myrrh with my spices.
I have eaten my honey comb with my honey.
    I have drunk my wine with my milk.

THE WOMEN OF JERUSALEM
Eat, friends, drink!
    Be intoxicated, lovers!

The poem in 4:1–7 relishes the woman's physical appearance from the top of her head to her breasts. The brief poem that follows (4:8–9) expresses the man's desire to be intimate with her; we treated it above in the chapter on desire. Now we pick up the man's description again in the present rapturous poem that begins once more with a general comment on beauty, this time the beauty of her love.

The Hebrew word translated as "love" here is less about the emotion and more about the physical act. The sensuous nature of this love is underlined by his comparing it favorably to wine. Wine tastes good, has a strong aftertaste, and leaves one a little heady.[5] The implication is that being in her embrace leaves him happy and lightheaded as well. Wine is not the only liquid that he uses to speak of her lovemaking. Honey and milk too are luxurious liquids that leave a strong aftertaste. These liquids, he poetically affirms, are under her tongue, implying his desire to taste the sweetness of her mouth with kisses.

He desires not only her taste but also her smell. Her oils (probably her perfume, but maybe her natural scent) are spicy and pleasing. Indeed, her smell is like that most pleasing scent of all, the smell of the cedars of Lebanon.

With that he comes to the climax of his description, languorously dwelling on her garden and the fountain in its midst. First, note how he speaks to her. He addresses her first as his sister. Again, this is strange and potentially offensive to a modern reader who may believe it sounds like incest. But nothing could be further from the truth. We know not only from this present context (and remember that the Bible strictly prohibits incest; see Lev. 18 and 20), but also from the use of this epithet in Egyptian love poems, that this is simply a term of endearment. He also refers to her as his "bride," placing these songs firmly in a marital context, perhaps even suggesting that they are the type of songs sung in anticipation of a bridal night.

But what about the garden and its fountain? What do they represent? It certainly is a most unusual and precious garden, filled with exotic spices. He devotes the longest section to the garden, lovingly spelling out its contents. While the image of the garden and the fountain in its midst is strange to us, the ancient reader knew it was a well-used metaphor for a woman's vagina.

Note that the woman's garden is "locked" and its fountain is "sealed." No one has yet penetrated her garden or tasted its fountain's waters. That said, one cannot miss the man's desire to enter this desirable place.

The man's description comes to an end, but the woman quickly responds to his unspoken desire. She opens her garden to her lover's entrance. She invites him to eat its choice fruit. The man's next words (5:1) indicate that he happily accepted her permission and now rejoices that he has been fully satisfied by her. The poem closes with the women of Jerusalem, the chorus of the Song, celebrating this most intimate of unions.

This Is My Lover (5:10–16)

THE WOMAN
My lover is radiant and ruddy,
  distinguished among ten thousand!
His head is pure gold.
  His locks are wavy, black like a raven.
His eyes are like doves by water streams,
  bathing in milk,
  sitting by pools.
His cheeks are like spice beds
  growing aromatics.
His lips are lilies
  dripping with liquid myrrh.
His arms are bars of gold,
  set with Tarshish-stones.
His member is an ivory tusk,
  ornamented with lapis.
His legs are pillars of marble,
  founded on gold pedestals.
His appearance is like Lebanon,
  choice like the cedars.
His palate is sweet.
  He is totally desirable.
This is my lover
  and this is my darling, O daughters of Jerusalem.

Now the woman describes the physical beauty of her husband, and her language is as provocative and erotic as his description of her. The broader context of this description is 5:2–6:3, which we will examine more fully in chapter 12. For now we concentrate on her passionate description of his appearance.

The woman believes that her lover stands out among all the other men. Even if there were ten thousand men standing in a group, her eyes would be attracted to him. His complexion is ruddy, a translation of a Hebrew word that suggests the swarthy complexion of a man from Israel. Whatever the exact hue of his complexion, she finds it scintillating.

As with the woman's description by the man in 4:1–7, her description begins with his head. Interestingly, she describes his head as "pure gold." The closest analogue in the Old Testament is the pure gold statue that Nebuchadnezzar puts up in the plain of Dura (Dan. 2). Indeed, much of the woman's description of the man sounds tantalizingly like the statue of a god. Certainly, she considers him a man and she does not worship him, but perhaps it is fair to say that he is king-like, if not god-like, in her eyes.

She now comments on his hair, black and wavy, as expected in a Hebrew man, and then his eyes, that like hers are compared to doves. Here though we have a more expansive description than we saw in 4:1. These doves are bathed in milk and thus suggest the pupil and iris of the eye surrounded by the whiteness of the rest of the eye. The reference to water in relationship to the eye indicates that they are glistening rather than dry. Whatever the exact significance of this description, the woman obviously finds his eyes mesmerizing.

Next his cheeks are described as spice beds, another odd metaphor for the modern reader. To picture it we have to remember that all adult men in Israel had a full beard. There were laws that prohibited the clipping of beards (Lev. 19:27), and shaving was embarrassing and unmanly (2 Sam. 10:4; Isa. 15:2). His cheeks grow a beard like a garden grows plants. They are spiced, indicating that he uses cologne, the pleasant smell of which invites physical intimacy.

How exactly his lips are like lilies is difficult for us to understand, but that they drip liquid myrrh indicates their desirability. There is no question that his lips arouse her desire.

His arms, like his head, are gold, ornamented by Tarshish stones. While we do not know exactly what such stones were, we do know that Tarshish is a faraway place, an exotic place. Indeed, many scholars believe that Tarshish is Spain, about as far as the imagination can run at the time the Old Testament was written. Perhaps this continues the statue-like description of the man that shows he is larger than life in her loving eyes. Perhaps it indicates that he wears armbands of gold. We cannot be sure.

Next she comments on his "member." Here most English translations prevaricate. The NIV, for instance, translates this as "his body is like

The Intrigue of Beauty

polished ivory decorated with lapis lazuli," even though the Hebrew word suggests an erogenous part of the body and the natural form of ivory (the tusk) suggests a particular part of the body, the member.

The reticence to straightforwardly translate arises from the idea that the Bible couldn't really be talking about a man's penis, could it, especially with a metaphor that seems to picture it as erect. It appears that we are more prudish than the Bible. If the man's description includes reference to the woman's breasts and vagina, why are we surprised or shocked that the woman delights in his erect penis?

The woman does not stop there, though, but continues down his body to refer to his legs, again continuing to picture him as a statue, made out of the most precious materials. She began with an overall picture of his appearance and thus she ends, comparing him to the beautiful, cedar-smelling region of Lebanon. Finally, his mouth's sweetness indicates that she wants to kiss it to enjoy its pleasant flavor.

I Will Climb the Palm Tree (6:13–7:10)

The Women of Jerusalem
Return, return, O Shulammite!
   Return, return, that we might look at you!

The Woman
Why should you gaze at the Shulammite,
   as the dance of two war camps?

The Man
How beautiful are your feet in sandals, O noble daughter!
   Rounded are your hips like rings,
      the work of the hands of a craftsman.
Your "navel" is a rounded bowl
   which does not lack mixed wine.
Your "belly" is a heap of wheat,
   bordered with lilies.
Your two breasts are like two fawns,
   twins of a gazelle.

Your neck is like an ivory tower.
    Your eyes are pools in Heshbon,
    by the gate of Bat-rabbim.
Your head . . . is like Carmel
    and the hair of your head like purple.
    The king is ensnared by your tresses.
How beautiful you are, and how pleasant,
    O love with your delights.
This—your stature—is like a palm tree,
    and your breasts are like fruit clusters.
I said, "I will climb up the palm tree;
    I will grasp its date blossoms!"
May your breasts be like clusters of the vine,
    and the smell of your breath be like apples.
May your palette be like fine wine,
    running straight to me,
    flowing over my lips and my teeth.

THE WOMAN

I belong to my lover,
    and his desire is for me.

The final descriptive poem of the Song is uttered by the man. Some of the descriptions are similar to those he already spoke in the earlier poem, but there are new, strikingly erotic depictions of the woman. Also note that, this time, the man starts his description from her feet and moves up her body with his loving compliments. After all, as the opening banter between the women of Jerusalem and the woman makes clear, she is dancing. They ask her to turn, to twirl, and she responds by asking why they are so fixed on her. She compares their gaze to that of the movements of two armies on the battlefield. While at first it may seem strange to us that she compares their watching her dance with a battle, we should imagine the scene of battle from a point overlooking the battlefield. As the two armies encountered one another, who could turn their eyes from the scene as they watched the strategic moves and countermoves of attack and defense? The beauty of the Shulammite draws the same kind of awestruck attention.

She is here called the Shulammite, and only here in the entire Song. Preceded by the definite article ("the"), Shulammite is not a personal name. It could refer to the village from which she came, but of more significance is the meaning of the name. Shulammite is formed from that common and well-known Hebrew word *shalom*. It is not coincidental that the only other person given a name in the Song is Solomon, whose name is also built on the same word, as the Hebrew version indicates (*Shelomo*). We will explore the significance of these names and their connection with peace or contentedness later (in chap. 16 when we deal with 8:8–12). For now, we will focus on his description of her beauty and how it moves him.

She is dancing, so he first notices her feet, calling them beautiful, before moving on to her undulating hips and then to her "navel" and "belly." The words are in quotation marks because they are almost certainly euphemisms for the woman's vagina. After all, the "navel" is said to be moist, as is the vagina when a woman is sexually excited. Even if the reference is to her navel, the man would find it arousing because of its proximity to her vagina and because it is suggestive of an actual opening. The description of the "navel" as containing wine implies the man's desire to drink from the sensual bowl. Thus, this may be a subtle and tasteful allusion to the intimacies of sex. The verse goes on to describe her "belly" as a heap of wheat. The image may not be visual but rather suggestive of fertility. If so, then more than her stomach is meant. We have here another tasteful reference to her vagina, the heap of wheat inviting comparison with her pubic hair. It is a work of art to the man, bordered by lilies.

While his earlier description pictured her neck as David's tower, a military fortress, here it is an ivory tower, again a martial image, one that indicates a strong, dignified, and perhaps elegant neck.

Historical distance obscures our understanding of the description of her eyes, since we don't know much about Heshbon and its pools that were near the gate of Bat-rabbim, but we can assume that they were renowned for their beauty. Moderns may laugh at the description of her nose also as a tower, but standards of beauty do not stay constant between cultures and time periods. Connecting the tower with Lebanon again brings up the pleasant smell of that region with its famous cedar forests.

She stands tall and dignified, just like Carmel, the mountain range that juts out into the Mediterranean. Her purple hair is metaphorical, purple being so expensive that only royalty could possess it. He is entranced by her hair; indeed, her stunning beauty cannot be resisted.

At this point, the lover takes a different approach in his description of her beauty, one that will lead to action on his part. He looks at her again and compares her to a palm tree, and specifically associates the fruit of the palm with her breasts. He then announces his intention to climb this palm tree and to grasp its fruit. It does not take much imagination to understand the suggestive sexual language as the man figuratively describes shimmying up the woman's body and fondling her breasts. He concludes by expecting her breath to be pleasant like apples and her mouth to taste like and give the same results (lightheadedness) as wine. The poem ends with the woman's happy acknowledgment that she and her lover are one.

The language of arousal in erotic beauty is breathtaking. It defies any form of ascetic piety or disembodied holiness. When we fail to be aroused by the physicality of our spouse we have turned away from being captured by God's creation. But what if our spouse is overweight? Aging? Or what if our spouse is not as physically attractive as the waitress delivering our pizza?

> The language of arousal in erotic beauty is breathtaking. It defies any form of ascetic piety or disembodied holiness.

Beauty—male or female, old or young, overweight or thin—is meant to capture our desire and delight. First, every culture defines what is beautiful, and any variance is seen as less attractive. This is a failure to see that every bit of creation bears the beauty of the Creator. There is beauty in every body, in every portion of creation. Second, beauty is bound not merely to sight but to the soul ("Charm is deceitful, and beauty is vain, but a woman who fears the LORD is to be praised," Prov. 31:30 NRSV). The more we delight in inner beauty, the more we will be readily disposed to be in awe of the beauty even in an aging person. We must grow in our ability to see the body as a reflection of the glory of the unseen.

8

After the
Bible Study on Beauty

think I finally figured out why so many Christians are freaked out about this book being in the Bible. I'm freaked. It is not that I am unfamiliar with erotica both in word and deed. I remember perusing my Dad's pornography when I was a scant eight years old. What I saw was nothing I had not seen when my mom was drunk on the couch.

Nakedness was a way station not a destination. I won't deny interest in arousal, but the intense rush of anticipation simmered to a warm, familiar pleasure. The passages we looked at embarrassed me when we read them out loud, in part due to the utter strangeness of some of the language: I'm not sure I'd ever thought about the erotic pleasure in knowing a woman has all her teeth, but then again . . . dental care does matter.

I couldn't take my eyes off the red blotches on Lois's neck. Her neck is like a radar—anytime we are swimming in dark waters, she lights up. And I don't know why, but when she gets flustered I feel awkward. I spent a lot of the night awkward until she finally spoke.

"These passages have ruined for me my last place of safety. I love gardens, and flowers have been one of the few things left for me to enjoy that isn't related to men, people, or sex. Now my garden feels like someone came through and ripped all the petals off and left a stinking aroma. I know I'm Debbie Downer, but this book really makes me miserable. The only times someone called me beautiful, it was the dues the dude had to pay to get my clothes off. And this is supposed to increase my heart for God? So far, it isn't happening."

No one spoke. I was stunned that Jill broke the silence. Of all people. That night she was wearing a silk bodice with white lace that showed slightly above her tight brown sweater. I noticed first her elegant necklace with a large opal that hung perilously above her cleavage. Like the man I met on my last trip to the Texas Panhandle whose shield of a belt buckle with rodeo figures sauntered over his groin. Both demanded that I not only notice but sneak looks.

If Celeste had spoken, I wouldn't have been surprised. She is a leader. She is lovely, but she doesn't demand that I sneak a look. She simply invites others to enjoy her. But Jill seems to be the polar opposite of Lois, and for her to jump into Lois's defiled garden seemed pretty risky.

"I know, Lois, you don't think I have a right to speak, let alone claim to understand what you're saying." Lois stared at her like a drunk college kid in the front row of a strip club, not sure whether to gawk or climb up on stage.

I thought Lois might deck her, but she said, "I want to hear what you have to say, Jill. Of anyone in this group, I've known all along you struggle with your body as much as me, and maybe even as much as Malcolm."

I almost didn't recognize my name. I looked at Lois and I thought she might have winked, or it might have been a tick. Jill laughed and tossed her head back, her chrome blond hair arcing like she was playing air guitar. Her neck was alabaster smooth, and she seemed younger than her years. I glanced at Marty and he looked like a cornered elephant trembling before a saucy mouse. I watched his chest to see if he was going to breathe. I had never seen him look more uncomfortable.

"Lois, you nailed it. I remember falling for the saccharine seductions when I was younger—it was so exciting when I actually believed the words were true and mattered, and then it became little more than a game. I let Marty woo me and he turns on his salesman charm and we both pretend that he means it and it matters to me. It's more like background muzak—it fills the air before you make the purchase."

Her eyes arched and she leaned toward Marty. She snapped, "Oh, take off that look of hurt. You know everything I said is true."

Marty stretched back to his full elastic self and smiled. "Well, am I wrong for simply following the Word of God and wanting to climb your tree and squeeze your melons?"

"Melons?" Amihan and Celeste spoke in union, full of incredulity and barely hidden disdain. The four women in the group had never been more united—you could feel the heat in the room swell. The sisterhood that had endured insufferable sexual innuendo, bad come-on lines, and blatant congratulatory remarks about their breasts brought them to stand against Marty as the symbol of all stupid sexual male blunders.

Brave Jon then stepped into the fray. I stood back and watched this show with both terror and utter fascination as Jon waded into the Rubicon. "We all take such a different angle when we read these passages. It sounds like you four women know something we three men need to hear. Let me say that I may never understand your level of anger and hurt, and I need to. But there are times, Celeste, when you seem to need to hear you are beautiful to me and other times that when I say you're beautiful, you look at me like I'm either stupid, lying, or manipulative. Obviously, I can be all three and maybe all at once, so I know there are things in our marriage I need to address. And I need to know more about where you feel cheapened by me or other men. But with all that noise in you and around you, you seem to be saying—you all seem to be saying—that nothing in this text moves you. What am I missing?"

I almost answered. Not that I know. I only feel at times like I am closer to a woman's soul than to a man's. I have read this war in the face of the women I have been with, even the women who stared back at me from two-dimensional pages.

Take me, want me—tell me I am ravishing. Tell me that no one has ever provoked your heart to beat as fast as I do. Don't turn from me to another. See only me.

But who can bear that consuming intensity and singularity of focus? I may want that intense intimacy for eternity but I can only endure it for a blink of the eye before I need space, distance from your overweening needs. As one woman said to me, "I like you because you don't need me. I get to be as needy as I want and you bring me wine and I never have to fear that you are actually willing to bleed for me."

Celeste said, "Jon, it won't be the first time I have confused you. I can't speak for women, only for me. I need to hear how you want to ravish me, but I fear your ravaging me. I need to know that you think I am beautiful, yet I also don't trust you a hundred percent when you tell me. Sometimes it's me; sometimes it is you. I know I'm not clear. I'm sorry, and I need you to know that believing I am beautiful is not easy."

Lois's eyes were brighter yet and even more intense. I wouldn't have ever said she is beautiful, but she was. If a Lois shines and no one sees her, is she beautiful? I don't know because I got to see her smile in the presence of other women. Each of them seemed to have battled in the beauty war. And each knew the cost of being beautiful and yet somehow not beautiful enough.

Beauty is physical, embodied, for sure. It is about breasts like dates and a penis that glistens with jewels. (Truly a weird image; I'd like to meet the woman who came up with that one.) And it is about the face: alive, bold, free, full of desire, tender, and kind. I am willing to say I am a Christian, sort of, but I am not willing yet to say that I want to be that kind of face or be with someone with that kind of beauty. At least I got to see a glimpse of it in Lois.

9

The Sad Sexual Tales
of My Friend

I ran into Amihan downtown today. She had forty-five minutes before she had to be at an appointment so we decided to grab coffee and talk. It was the first time I realized that not only am I fond of her, but I have come to like the sex group. They are disturbed and kind people. This feels as humbling to confess as admitting that I am more aroused by older women.

Amihan was relaxed and playful without any degree of flirtation. She laughed about each person in the group but in a way that if they had been present, they would have been more honored than embarrassed. She talks mostly with her left hand. Her lips move in a syncopated rush, percussive and direct, but her hand sways like the big band sounds of the swing era. Her skin is smooth, flawless. Her thin, dark eyebrows rise and fall like the gentle lapping of water on an ocean beach, and when she gets slightly intense her eyes focus with crystalline clarity.

She poked me in the arm.

"Malcolm, stop reading my face. You're too young for me and I am too young for you."

I'm usually more suave in that kind of repartee with a woman, but I just stared at her and blushed.

"I know, but your face and hands say as much if not more than your words."

It was a lame reply but true. I just couldn't keep my eyes off her expressive face. I loved having been caught, yet with the freedom to laugh together. It made me so grateful that we were coconspirators about sex without any of the burdensome flirtation or the awkwardness of trying to get up in the morning and explain what happened the night before. This actually feels good.

Amihan told me she has been on a Christian online dating service and had another date last night. Her complexion changed to a fiery hue and her eyes were no longer placid and playful. I felt like she had instantaneously put on her SWAT-team armor and applied the dark streaks of a game face.

Apparently, she had dated this guy for about eight weeks. She had been up front in her profile and in their first conversations that she didn't intend to have sex until she was married. Each man she met on the site concurred and vowed the same. But each man in the third or fourth date made sexual overtures that could easily have led to full-blown whoopee. She deferred and they apologized, but each date after that the same drill occurred, until the men faded to invisibility and refused to answer their phone or respond to email.

Christian dating is about taking a stand that everyone knows is absolute—until the third date. The dude she was with last night tried to get her to stay overnight.

"It is such a long way back to your place, and if we want to finish the movie it will be so much easier if you sleep over and get up early in the morning. I'll sleep in the guest room, and if you need to feel more comfortable you can lock the door."

As a long time seducer I found such gyrations puerile. She deserves far more than the bid to spend the night. I tried to find a more Christian way to say it but it still came out distorted.

"Amihan, you deserve a better man, who at least knows how to be less predatory."

Somehow my words just made her laugh. "Malcolm, you are still such a hybrid pagan boy and wistful old man." I blushed again.

She told me that they had a long discussion about why she was not making it beyond the six-week barrier in her dating. She was actually serious about remaining a virgin. The dude told her that as long as she failed to put out at least in the first six weeks, then she was going to be left out.

This man was actually trying to be kind, to let her know the unspoken rules about Christian dating. The only real difference between religious and secular men is the timeline. Christians are hypocritical on the front end, guilty in the postlude, and then use moral failure as the basis for the eventual breakup. Pagans are more honest—it's about the sex.

I am a pagan boy trying to find my way in my new tribe, and I find it disorienting to be with seducers whose craft is not well developed. To think he would use the "I will sleep in the other bedroom" ruse with a straight face gives me hives. But I appreciate his honesty about the timeline, his admission that if sex doesn't happen within the "passion just took over our moral sensibilities" time limit, you are kaput. At least he took her into his magic vault and showed her how the sleight-of-hand tricks are done.

But it led to a good discussion with Amihan about the sexual games that mark her dating. It is a maze of ridiculous, hilarious, and heartbreaking stories of men feeding her the same bobbled lines, muffed endearments, and bollixed pawing. As a Christian who is not sure what to do with his sexuality, I certainly don't want to pander to such well-worn folderol.

She shared some of the lines she has heard.

"I have never been with a more beautiful woman than you."

"I feel more alive with you than I have ever felt with any other person in my life."

"You make my heart skip like a fawn."

"You are so hot. Sexy. Erotic. Sexy hot."

I could cry or scream. My favorite line she shared was that she was "more delicious than lubricious." It is something that Rilke might say if he was stupid drunk.

We are all fragments of our earliest lusts and injudicious experimentation, let alone our past infidelities and harm of others—fine virgin wool and greasy cheap polyester woven together into a ludicrous zigzag flame pattern. I am not ashamed of my sexual stories, trysts, peccadilloes, infatuations, or fantasies as much as I am embarrassed that the sum total seems so vacuous.

I am sure there is shame written somewhere in and below the surface, but after hearing Amihan tell of the pathetic squalor of her seducers I am left wondering again how poems from the Bible can make sex more than the empty thing it seems to be in both my old world and this new one. I am glad this coming week will resolve all my questions about how to think about sex in a God-honoring and life-giving way rather than listing back and forth and feeling either stoned indifferent or nauseous.

I am trying to fight the low, rumbling bile of the cynicism that rises in my throat when I think about sex. I am no longer downing Tums to whittle down the angst and emptiness. I can't purge this feeling through more sex like I used to do. I am in such a quandary—give in to the dark judgments, surrender to sensuality to neutralize the acid, or what? Sex is so sad when one doesn't have the benefit of alcohol or predatory indifference. Enough. Enough. Enough for now.

10

The Fantasy of Sexual Play

We are beings who live and breathe, think and feel, plot and plan, deduce and learn through narrative. We are not simply sexual beings; we are sexual beings who live out our sexuality through stories and fantasies of desire and beauty.

Our sexuality is always shaped and guided by scripts that are more complex than the software code that directs the hardware of a computer. We unwittingly inherit sexual scripts from our body, our family, the culture, the church, our friends, pornography, past sexual abuse, and countless other sources. And we shape those conscious and unconscious scripts with our later edits and additions throughout our lives. We are fearfully and wonderfully complex beings who can never be fully understood or explained. All of us have both internal scripts and fantasies that influence how we engage and experience our sexual desires and actions.

There are four common scripts or fantasies that guide most people's sexual arousal: scripts of intimacy, variety, power, or violation of taboo. Intimacy includes story elements that honor oneself and one's partner while also increasing pleasure and care. Variety involves scenes that intensify arousal due to a change in the setting, process, or persona related to arousal. Power is either taking over another through desire or physical force or relinquishing to another, freeing oneself from the burden of choice or honor. And finally, there is an immense realm of fantasy that involves varying degrees of crossing the boundaries of a family or culture. Sex is not merely about erogenous pleasure; it is also about mapping out individual terrain of what is going to be considered shameful and taboo versus beautiful and life giving.

These four categories reveal that sexual stories serve to aid intimacy, escape boredom, negotiate power, and define our identity both inside and outside our community. Fantasy structures can enable us to better honor our partners and help us understand the impulse of our arousal, or they can pervert love and turn us away from our lover in our secrecy and shame.

"Script" is an apt word to use for our discussion. It implies a play with setting, characters, dialogue, action, and movement in a scene that is meant to capture our attention and quicken our intrigue. We are both observers/spectators who see this scene and participants who are allowed some distance from the action. We are not merely being informed; we are being invited to lose ourselves, to a degree, in the play.

Like all good storytelling, from novels to films, we are both in and not of a process. If it is a compelling poem, we are entranced, beguiled by the words and images, and lost in the drama set before us, and afterward, we may allow the images, words, or even just the ambience of the movement to be factored into our internal thoughts and actions.

Consider the power of pornography as a form of sexual script or fantasy. Research indicates that the brain is virtually seared by the high dopamine levels that the images of pornography elicit. The brain is flooded with the same kind of pleasure as when exposed to cocaine or heroin. Our brains respond to those images with amazing intensity, whether desired or not at the time, and continue to do so even later, in spite of grief or shame. (Images constructed by words rather than pictures or direct observation do not have the same "searing" power.)

In sum, most sexual fantasies are not a mere replay of direct sexual experience but a series of images or scenes woven from past experience, desire, observation, and outright creative imagination.

Amazingly to some, the Bible is inviting us to fantasize and begin to form categories for sexual play. The Bible does not assume that we encounter sexual arousal or stories for the first time upon finding ourselves married. Our sexuality does not lie dormant and then suddenly arise on our wedding day. We are sexual beings from birth, and we are part of sexual narratives from our first day of life, if not before.

It is naive to think that children are not curious and experimenting from their first year. Their experimentation lacks cognizance or shame at first, but as lessons are learned about gender difference, family and cultural norms, and individual desire, more and more awareness grows that sexuality is a defining personal and relational issue. Add to that volatile mix our culture's sexual indulgence, fears, and the vast intrusion of sexuality into the elementary school years by the media and advertising, and it is impossible to avoid a child's early development of sexual scripts. Further add sexual abuse and early sexual adventurism—let alone playground taunts, seductions, and accusations—and our volatile inner world becomes a life-shaping drama.

> Amazingly to some, the Bible is inviting us to fantasize and begin to form categories for sexual play.

Sadly, we seldom reflect on all this. Most often we either indulge or fight these scripts. We tend to follow the narrative road or try to find ways to escape it through therapy, self-control, or punitive violence. More often than not, our silence and refusal to reflect on our internal script only strengthens the power of its unseen, unaddressed, unconscious meanings, therefore keeping us bound to our script even when we are desperate to change it.

To summarize, we are sexual beings that are aroused and moved by sexual stories and scripts that most often remain internal and secretive and at times even hidden from ourselves. We can no more escape our internal sexual stories than we can flee from being sexual.

The Bible offers us windows into sexual scenes that are meant to shape our fantasies and direct our way of being sexual with our spouse. The poems offered are not meant to be the only guides or the only acceptable fantasies, but they offer a normative picture of what constitutes sexual scenes and stories that are pleasing to the body and to the God who created our bodies.

Intimate Fragrances (1:12–14)

THE WOMAN
While the king is on his couch
    my nard gives off its scent.
My lover is to me a sachet of myrrh
    lodging between my breasts.
A cluster of henna blossoms is my lover to me
    in the vineyards of En-gedi.

The woman speaks and describes a moment of great intimacy with her beloved. The poem describes the initiation of lovemaking as she pictures herself reclined on a couch with the man's head cradled between her breasts.

She wears perfume that smells like nard, a plant whose roots can be crushed and made into an oil that is pleasantly aromatic. The plant is found in India and was extremely expensive. Lovemaking involves all the senses, and in this poem the emphasis is on smell. Perfumes arouse not only the senses but also the emotions, and they invite closeness. Her metaphor of her beloved as a sachet of myrrh suggests that he too is perfumed. Myrrh is rare and expensive and comes from an aromatic gum that exudes from the bark of a tree that grows in Arabia, Abyssinia, and India.

They are on a couch that allows them to lie down together as they embrace. The final verse names yet another aromatic plant, henna and its blossoms. Henna is a shrub that grows in Egypt and Palestine. But this is no ordinary henna; it came from En-gedi. While a number of the geographical references in the Song of Songs are unknown to us today, En-gedi is familiar to anyone who has visited Israel as one of the most beautiful places in the world.

En-gedi is located on the western shore of the Dead Sea, just north of Masada, which was not yet built at the time the Song was written. The area around the Dead Sea is desolate in the extreme, a veritable salt waste. The ground is barren, and through much of the year it is subject to burning heat. En-gedi is a lush oasis in the midst of this stark land. Walking into this oasis we encounter a magnificent waterfall that fills a pool that provides a sheltered and warm, but not hot, environment. The atmosphere invites one to take clothes off and plunge into the pleasant waters. The poet's invocation of this wondrous location is, of course, intentional, as a place that beckons lovers to play in the midst of the uninviting wider surroundings.

Indeed, biblical scholars have seen in the reference to En-gedi an evocation of the Garden of Eden. We know the Garden of Eden as the place where the first man and the first woman were "naked and not ashamed" as they enjoyed each other, body and soul.

Flowers and Trees (2:1–7)

THE WOMAN
I am a flower of Sharon,
    a lily of the valleys.

THE MAN
Like a lily between thorns
    is my darling among the girls.

THE WOMAN
Like an apple tree among the trees of the forest
    is my lover among boys.
I desire his shade and I dwell there;
    his fruit is sweet to my palate.
He has brought me to the wine house,
    and his banner over me was "Love."
Sustain me with raisin cakes;
    refresh me with apples,
    for I am faint with love.
His left hand is under my head,
    and his right embraces me.
I adjure you, daughters of Jerusalem,
    by the gazelles or the deer of the field,
    not to awaken or arouse love until it desires.

This playful song opens with the woman demurely comparing herself to "a flower of Sharon, a lily of the valleys." The Hebrew word for "flower" certainly points to something beautiful, but also rather common. The word only occurs elsewhere in the Old Testament in Isaiah 35:1, where the

picture is the wilderness bursting forth with flowers. The different translations lead to radically different assessments of the woman's comment,
especially if read from a twenty-first-century perspective. After all, there
are few flowers as spectacular as the rose. If that is the right translation,
the woman is proclaiming herself stunningly beautiful, which seems a
bit presumptuous if not arrogant.

But she is not presumptuous. It is not as if she disowns her beauty.
Flowers are beautiful, no matter what kind of flower one is talking about.
But a rose is special. No, the woman is saying she is beautiful, but no
more so than other women. Sharon is a valley that is just between the
coast and the foothills of western Israel, north of Jaffa up to Athlit. The
reference to this area concretizes the imagery. In the spring this valley is
wild with flowers. In the second part of the verse, she specifies that she
is a lily, again a beautiful but rather common flower.

The main significance of her self-reference is that she is indeed pretty,
but not uncommonly so. To be sure, she does not deny her flower-like
attractiveness, but she is nothing special. She seems to imply that she is
not worthy of the man. There are plenty like her.[1]

If her comments are intended to elicit a compliment from him, they
succeed. The man responds by contradicting her modest claims. Interestingly, he still compares her to the lily, a rather ordinary flower. However,
by saying that she is a lily among thorns, he is saying she is indeed special.
To him, she is a flower and all the other women are thorns.

The thorn is not attractive compared to the flower, and certainly does
not invite intimacy or touch. The emphasis needs to be on his evaluation
of her. The woman is right that there are many, many beautiful women
in the world, but the man asserts that this particular woman attracts all
of his attention. To him, she is the only one worth looking at, the only
one with whom he wants to be intimate.

The woman now responds, showing that her feelings match his. She
too turns to the world of vegetation to talk about how special he is to
her. Rather than flowers, she compares him to a tree. He is an apple tree
among the trees of the forest. The other boys are like ordinary trees; he
is like the fertile, sweet-smelling apple tree.

She then expresses her desire to be intimate with him by saying that
she wants to dwell in the shade of her apple tree. She doesn't submit to

cultural flight from arousal or desire. She invites him to intimacy while maintaining a sense of autonomy in her desire that allows her arousal to intensify.[2] Her specific desire for physical intimacy is expressed by her statement that the apples of this tree are sweet to her taste. Significantly, the apple tree has persisted through the centuries as an erotic image.

After these enticing compliments that are a kind of verbal foreplay, the woman reports that he has brought her into the wine house. Already wine has been linked with lovemaking. Indeed, in 1:2 the woman passionately exclaims, "Your love is better than wine."

While their lovemaking is private, his proclamation of his passion for her is not. He speaks of publicly proclaiming his love for her by placing a banner over her that announces to one and all his feelings toward her. In this way, he says "she belongs to me; I am committed to her." Elsewhere in the Bible, particularly in the book of Numbers (1:52; 2:2, 3 and throughout), the banner is found in a military context. Banners were emblems that were set up in the war camp and carried by an army unit in battle. Here we have a military image used in the service of love (see also Ps. 45, the other love poem in the Bible, particularly vv. 3–5). In effect, it pictures the man as a soldier who is willing to fight on behalf of his love for her.

Their love is so strong and their lovemaking so passionate that she needs sustenance. After all, love can wear one out both emotionally and physically. She calls for raisin cakes and apples not only because she is drained but also because she wants to continue in their intimacy.

Verse 6 pictures them finally in a restful but intimate embrace. The passionate lovemaking may be over, but they rest in each other's arms at the end. The poem ends with an instruction to the group of young women who are the friends and disciples of the woman, but we will reserve explanation until later (see chap. 12).

A Poem of Spring (2:8–17)

THE WOMAN
The sound of my lover!
    See, he is coming,
    leaping over the mountains,
    bounding over hills!

My lover is like a gazelle
  or a young stag.
He is now standing behind our wall,
  staring through the window,
   peeking through the lattice.
My lover responded and said to me,
"Rise up, my darling,
  my beautiful one, and come, . . .
For now the winter has passed,
  the rains have come, gone.
Blossoms appear in the land.
  A time of singing has arrived,
   and the sound of the turtledoves is heard in our land.
Rise up, my darling,
  my beautiful one, and come. . . .
My dove, in the crevices of the rock,
  in the hiding place in the cliff,
let me see your form!
  Let me hear your voice!
For your voice is agreeable,
  and your form is pleasant."
"Grab the foxes,
  the little foxes!
They are ruining the vineyards,
  our vineyards in bloom."
My lover is mine and I am his;
  he grazes among the lilies.

  The garden setting of this poem again evokes memory of Eden—the time when the man and the woman were naked and felt no shame. They enjoyed each other fully and without obstacle, not only physically but also emotionally and spiritually. The setting reminds us again that the Song of Songs is about the redemption of sexuality.

  The time is the spring. The winter is over and now the spring has come. The spring is a time for new birth and explosive fertility. Spring is a time to take clothes off and cavort in newly arrived warmth.

  The woman speaks in this poem. She excitedly announces the sudden appearance of her beloved. In the Hebrew her opening words are brief, almost breathless in her passion. She describes his movement, which communicates his corresponding eager passion. After all, he is leaping and bounding, not just walking or even running. He moves like a gazelle, implying a swift agility. These opening lines indicate excitement and eagerness on both their parts. The description of his path to her as surmounting mountains symbolizes that the path is not without effort and obstacle, yet he easily comes into her presence seeking union.

Even so, when he arrives, they don't immediately embrace. They are not yet together. He stands outside the house in which she dwells. He looks through the window and urges her to come with him. He wants to eliminate all barriers between them and to be together in bliss.

As we remarked in our opening comments, the time is right. It is spring, the winter is over, the rains are finished. The flowers burst into bloom, spreading their fragrance. Death has passed; life stirs. Darkness is past; resurrection is now.

Shifting poetic imagery, the man now describes their distance by picturing her hiding in the crevice of a rock. In the Psalms, God is pictured as a rock in which we find protection (Pss. 18:2, 31; 19:14; 28:1). But no protection from the man is needed; to be with him is ecstasy. He wants to see her, hear her, touch her, smell her.

In what at first seems like a strange intrusion into her rhapsody of anticipated desire, he urges that they capture the foxes. We will explore the full significance of his words (as repeated by the woman) in chapter 12, but for now we note that there are dangers that need to be navigated in this garden of love. Intimacy, even redeemed, is not easy in this life. Obstacles present themselves. Even so, love is possible this side of heaven in spite of sin, according to the woman, who ends this poem by happily celebrating their mutual ownership: "My lover is mine and I am his."

Summary

It is impossible to feel desire for your spouse or any other person and not enter the realm of story. The story is usually made up of one or many scenes, just as we have found in these poems. Even when the arousal is focused on a single pornographic photo, the human mind takes the image and puts it into some kind of narrative. In that sense we are not aroused by mere sight or symbols; we are narrative beings who are brought to fulfillment through story.

It is tragic when a man requires his wife to wear a schoolgirl's outfit so he can be aroused at the story of seducing a young girl. It is no different with a nurse's uniform or other fantasy attire, or if the person you are fantasizing with is not your spouse.

What is the story that is guiding one's lovemaking? For many couples it is too dangerous to tell the other where one's thoughts go or what images are sustaining the arousal. And it is not our suggestion that those images be wantonly shared with one another.

> Shared fantasy, remembered goodness, and the sweetness of sexual joy are meant to help us anticipate the story of redemption.

What is our concern is whether the images and the story cause each partner to grow in delight and honor both for oneself and for the other. And even better if it is a shared story and one that gives each partner a context for understanding what lovemaking means at that moment for them.

One couple talked about making love after he had lost his job. His wife told him, "I know you feel violated by a boss that just dumped you, but when we make love I hope you remember when we were carefree and young and made love by that mountain lake." She was offering a time of lovemaking that was more innocent and free, and that called him to anticipate a better day ahead.

Shared fantasy, remembered goodness, and the sweetness of sexual joy are meant to help us anticipate the story of redemption. Every moment of sexual struggle and joy is a call to remember what we have known of goodness and what we anticipate ahead.

11

Before the
Bible Study on Struggles

Another confession: I don't dread going to the study. I look forward to seeing everyone each week, and somehow I like being part of their lives. Further confession: as we studied the scenes and the playful eroticism of the lovers' delight, I could only remember stories of harm.

Lois, that crafty fox, asked me during the sex-scenes discussion if there were any scenes or stories in my sexual history that brought me joy. I didn't divert or make a joke. I looked at her and said, "No. Plenty of pleasure, a few moments of connection, but nothing close to what I think might be the experience of joy."

Again, I feel haunted by my history. The scenes that remain revolve around what I suspect we are going to get into in the next study: conflict. My sexual story is a long slide into hurt. Either I am about to be used like a toy or I am going to hurt someone because I don't care.

I am not proud of this, but I got drunk a few nights ago and smoked some pot that was probably laced with psilocybin. I didn't intend to drink more than a couple of beers, but I ended up drinking a six-pack. And then I slipped off a chair into a circle of tokers and got handed a phenomenal cigar-like joint and proceeded to stop thinking about Jesus, sex, the study, my screwed-up life, and everything else except the compelling way lights seemed to stumble over each other and make strange arcs around the room.

Life was good until I needed to throw up. I found an out-of-the-way closet toilet, locked the door, and put my face on the cool, smooth porcelain. I threw up a few times, made a vow I wouldn't drink again for at least a month, and lowered my head down to the white bolts that kept the throne aright.

And then I dreamt, or hallucinated. It seemed I was in a gallery of portraits, mostly the Dutch Masters, with frilled collars, long necks, and pinched cheeks. I floated from one wing of the gallery to the next. Every now and then I'd recognize a face, and my feet would hover inches above the floor as I looked at the portrait. The face was usually of someone I am reluctant to call an abuser. Likely the only reason I could name the girls in the neighborhood, the older teenager on the beach, my eighth-grade teacher, and others as abusers is that I was stoned out of my mind. It was the final portrait that caused me to smack my head on the bottom of the toilet. My mom.

I have always liked the story of *A Christmas Carol* and Scrooge's midnight ride into truth—past, present, and future. I suspect it was because it was the only Christmas tradition I established in my parents' home other than Dad overspending on his mistresses and mom pouring rum into eggnog like it was water. I wanted the hallucination to turn into a Scrooge-like awakening to a brand-new future. It didn't.

The portraits were mute, even the one of my mom. She looked at me with a fierce expression that cut through me. I had the sense of being overwhelmed by rushing water. I remember her eyes almost always feeling unreadable, sphinxlike until she had her five o'clock reward for living through another pointless day. For the next few hours her face had color and her eyes were hungry. Mostly for me. I was her solace and the bait she used to mock and tease my father as she venerated me and lauded me in her drunken praise. I was everything a woman could want in contrast to his narcissistic bilge.

Then her eyes would slowly lose intensity, even mockery, and descend into a dull stare. When Lois asked if I had ever known sexual joy, I inadvertently remembered my mother's portrait in the gallery. I don't ever remember a single moment of sexual violation, but then why did her face hover when the question was asked?

I heard too much about sex from her. I saw her indelicately dressed more times than I can count. That can't be that troubling, given everything else I have experienced. All I know is that when her eyes feasted upon me, fierce, cutting, I ran like a madman to escape that prison bathroom.

A couple of days later, yesterday in fact, I read the section we are to read for the conflict study. What I walked away with is that the woman is willing to go hunt for her man late at night, apparently only something that prostitutes do, and then she gets abused by the police but is undaunted and keeps looking. As if that is not weird and awful enough, the next poem for the study is about her brothers mocking her for having small breasts and making her work in the fields to make her skin darker so she is less attractive. The police abuse and families meddle. That about summarizes it.

I just have to say I don't feel as weird about my sexual history as I read the Bible. In fact, I wonder if it is the articulation of the conflict and abuse that gives me the sense that the Bible is true. There is an honesty even in this poetry that gives me hope that I might be able to tell the truth too. Not to the group, not about my mom, and maybe not without a dollop of psilocybin.

12

The Struggle toward Intimacy

Part 1

The Song of Songs has often been characterized as an out-and-out celebration of sexual pleasure. As we have seen, the vast majority of the poems that make up the book live up to that billing. Indeed, in the conclusion we will see that the Song is really part of a biblical theology of sexuality that begins in the Garden of Eden.

In Genesis 2, Adam and Eve stand naked in each other's presence and feel no shame. However, once they sin by eating from the fruit of the tree, they immediately cover themselves. In the Song, the man and the woman can once again stand in a (poetic) garden and feel no shame—at least most of the time.

The Song presents a beautiful picture of God's precious gift of sexuality as something to be treasured and enjoyed, but it is also a realistic book. That is, it acknowledges that, though sex is a gift from God, intimacy—whether physical, emotional, or spiritual—is not easily achieved or sustained on this side of heaven.

Remember the little foxes mentioned in the last poem we treated in the previous chapter. In the midst of the man's idyllic rhapsody about spring in the garden of love, he unexpectedly shouts,

Grab the foxes,
   the little foxes!
They are ruining the vineyards,
   our vineyards in bloom. (2:15)

Who are these foxes? What do they represent? Most likely, the specific referent to this metaphor is intended to be vague and ambiguous. Or to put it more positively, the foxes stand for anything or anyone who threatens the harmony and well-being of the vineyard garden. That is, anything or anyone who presents danger to the intimate relationship between the man and the woman.

A fox is a pest that in ancient literature as well as in our day is a shrewd adversary and nearly impossible to catch. To be told to catch a fox is like being told to go catch a professional, *Ocean's Eleven*–style thief. It is not accomplished by setting up a sign that says, "No thieves are welcome here." In the same way, keeping the vineyard safe from harm requires immense wisdom and intense vigilance. To preserve sexual joy one must have the perseverance of a gardener who daily weeds her garden and the wisdom of the serpent, thereby outfoxing the foxes in protecting her hard-earned grapes.

> It acknowledges that, though sex is a gift from God, intimacy is not easily achieved or sustained on this side of heaven.

And what is the threat? The threat is relational, cultural, and spiritual. It is possible for the threat to come with malicious intent, perhaps someone who wants to break up the lovers' relationship for his or her own advantage, perhaps a rival suitor or someone who alienates the affections of a married person. It could be a friend who subtly undermines your marriage by inviting you to discontent or judgment of your spouse.

The threat is also cultural and embedded in our language. I (Dan) recently had a fishing guide who referred to his wife as "the wife." I asked him why he used the article "the," and he said, "I guess because she tries to run my life and 'the' gives me a little distance from her." Brilliant. He understood how language can be used to create distance or intimacy. It is common for women to conspire in frustration about "men" and equally for men to shrug their shoulders and speak derisively about "women."

Ultimately, if one acknowledges a spiritual realm, then that implies the conviction that there are "spirits" that serve God or serve God's enemy, the evil one. The assumption, then, should be obvious: evil despises what God loves. God loves sex. God loves sex that brings honor and joy in his kingdom. God loves good sex. Therefore, it is not just through pornography, immorality, seduction, and violence that evil works its darkness, but through any spirit that compromises joy. "Foxes" cover any realm that destroys the fruit of the vine.

> It is not just through pornography, immorality, seduction, and violence that evil works its darkness, but through any spirit that compromises joy.

But the foxes could be benign as well. When I (Tremper) ask classes of young married couples to identify the "foxes" that threaten the intimacy of their marriages, without hesitation most say "children." But the possibilities for the identification of the foxes are endless, and the principle is clear: there are forces, people, things that make it difficult to achieve the physical intimacy celebrated in the Song.

The reference to the foxes is not the only place that the Song of Songs acknowledges the difficulty of relationship. One of the most gripping is the poem found in 5:2–6:3. The poem is long, so we will take it section by section.

THE WOMAN
I was sleeping, but my mind was alert.
The sound of my lover knocking!
"Open for me, my sister, my darling,
my dove, my flawless one.
My head is full of dew;
my locks with the drizzle of the night." (5:2)

The woman is in her bed for the night. Some take the reference to her alert mind as an indication that she is dreaming and that what follows is a dream sequence. If it is a dream sequence, then it highlights even more the fact that it is not a time-and-space story that follows a narrative arc.

Even if it is not a dream, it is important to highlight that it is a poem and not a story. There are a number of transitions that simply do not make any sense if it is seen as a description of an actual event. This passage contains figurative language, some of it quite well known from other ancient poems.

One of the initial images is the door of the woman's house. In this poem, the man and the woman are married, and so a prosaic reader might ask, Why is the man's wife in a separate house? Why does the man have to come to her house to have sex? But this question is the wrong one to ask. The right question is, What does the door stand for?

An ancient Israelite reader would know right away. The door stands for the woman's vagina. We will also see this use of the door image in 8:9 as part of a passage to be treated below. Thus, he is asking for entrance into the woman. He wants her to open up to him sexually. He is asking for sexual intimacy.

It is harder to be certain what we are to make of the man's physical condition as he stands at the door. Perhaps it indicates his readiness for sex, but at the very least it shows that he has come through uncomfortable conditions to be with her. His desire has propelled him through the rain with the hope of seeking her warmth. If so, he is soon to suffer disappointment.

> I have taken off my clothes,
> should I get dressed again?
> I have washed my feet,
> should I get them dirty? (5:3)

While the man moves toward the woman with desire for intimacy, her first reaction is to move away from him. Her excuse is framed in questions. We know quickly the difference between a question that asks for information and a question that is a thinly veiled accusation. She has settled down for the night. She is in bed and does not want to get dressed again. (But does he want her to get dressed? Certainly not.) She does not want to walk across the floor to open the door for him.

In the ancient Near East, the word "feet" often is a euphemism for genitals. Most certainly she is saying to him, "Do you really want me to be soiled by your sperm?"

> My lover sent his hand through the hole,
>   and my innards roiled toward him. (5:4)

Here the poet uses double entendre in describing the man as he seeks access through the door, presumably by working the lock. Hands (like feet) in the Bible, and in the broader culture of the ancient Near East, can represent the penis. He is trying to initiate sexual relations (though on the surface level of the poem he is still outside). It is not that he is trying to force sex on the reluctant woman, but rather he is taking her reply as a tease.

However we are to understand the man's actions here precisely, there is no doubt about the woman's response. She is becoming aroused, innards here a rather inelegant translation of a word that means her erogenous zone. She is becoming sexually aroused. Thus, she now moves toward him.

> I stood up to open to my lover,
>   and my hands dripped myrrh
>   and my fingers liquid myrrh
>   on the handles of the lock.
> I opened to my lover,
>   but my lover had gone away; he had left.
>   My spirit had gone out at his speaking. (5:5–6a)

He had asked her to open the door to him, and now that she is aroused, she does so. When she seizes the door to open it her hands are wet with myrrh. The picture likely expresses the extent of her arousal. She is not just vaginally ready, but her hands drip with her arousal.

The image draws us to anticipate more than mere pleasure and orgasm; it evokes the deep hunger of the heart to be ravenously desired. For many people passionate sex is a lost dream found only through the lonely fantasies of pornography. Others find a counterfeit passion through the haze of alcohol. It is the rare couple that knows both intense desire and delight. It appears in the text that sensual joy is about to happen.

However, now it is her turn to be disappointed. As she opens up to her lover, she stares into open space. He thought she was not interested, and now that she is, he has already left. Her reaction ("my spirit had gone out at his speaking") expresses bewilderment, confusion, and sadness. However, she may be disappointed, but she is not passive.

> I sought him, but did not find him.
>> I called him, but he did not answer.
> The guards found me,
>> those who make their rounds in the city.
> They struck me; they bruised me.
>> They lifted my garments from me,
>> those guards of the walls. (5:6b–7)

Rather than return to her bed, she sets out in search of her lover. Her initial attempts to find him fail. He is nowhere to be found. But still she goes out in pursuit.

Soon she encounters danger and harm. In one of the most heart-wrenching scenes in the book, she encounters the city guards (the police). She is, after all, a woman alone and out at night looking for a man.

Perhaps they suspect she is a prostitute, and so they beat her; they sexually assault and degrade her ("they lifted my garments from me"). It is easy for modern readers to get stuck at this point. She is a woman being beaten and sexually violated by the police. We are enraged, but, as we will see, the woman ignores them and just moves on with her search. How are we to understand this?

This poem uses a culturally dark reality to intensify how much risk she is willing to take to be united to her lover, but it also exposes how easy it is to ignore sexual harm.

First, we must remember again that this is a poem, not a literal description of an actual event. The proper question to ask is, What do the guards represent? How are we to understand their use in this passage?

The best interpretation understands the guards to represent the social customs or assumptions of the day. Notice first of all how the woman's assault is not a big deal to her. There are at least several issues to be considered. Violence against women was seldom considered to be noteworthy in the ancient world. This poem uses a culturally dark reality to intensify how much risk she is willing to take to be united to her lover, but it also exposes how easy it is to ignore sexual harm. As readers, we are meant to be disturbed by both the nonchalance of the violence and, equally, the intensity of her desire.

The poet comes close to saying the woman's passion puts her in danger of being seen as a prostitute. In risking this misperception the poet is also exposing the violence of men against a woman fueled by desire for power. Tragically, this is a sentiment that is often acted out in violence of word and deed against women in all cultures to this day. Sexual experience is an expected rite of passage for boys, and yet for girls sexual desire comes with physical and verbal degradation equivalent to the assault of the woman by the guards in the above passage.

We are to read then the "police" as the guardians of female sexuality who are intensely committed to controlling it while also drawn to use and degrade a sexuality they don't understand. How very different are the guards from the man of the Song of Songs who stands and waits at the door, while the guards break through her wall even though they are meant to be guardians of the gate.

One only need consider the nature of pornography to see the arc of violence against women. Women are overwhelmingly the targets of both verbal and physical violence and aggression in pornography. However, whether due to greater awareness of sexual assault, greater regard for women, a sense of conscience, or something else, there has been an interesting shift in pornography away from depictions of unwilling women being sexually dominated. Rape of an unwilling woman isn't as sexy as it used to be for the mainstream porn consumer, and the porn industry has listened and thus created scenes where women, though still targets of violence, are depicted as not resisting the aggression and in fact as experiencing pleasure, a supposed mark of their willingness, which then allows for erasure of any label of violence. Unfortunately, the shift has only been a dark and subtle turn meant to both preserve and avoid the categories of violence or aggression in order to maintain arousal, where response rather than action has become the measure of whether an act is violent or not.[1]

If so-called soft porn offers the traditional come-hither look that invites the fantasy of being wanted, then harder-core pornography inevitably moves toward a man, or more often a woman, being degraded in some form. The darkest pornography involves the intersection of humiliation and violence, even to the extent of taking human life as a sacrifice to a man's ultimate desire for power.

The poet subtly exposes the darkness of male lust, fear, and degradation. And he uses it to say that a woman with desire for her lover is not ignorant of violence against her, nor does this violence ultimately foul her desire. The man may have endured the drizzle of the night as he approached her, but now the woman will endure even more—moving through the violence of those who do not know what to do with female sexuality—for the sake of finding intimacy with the man. But she needs help, so she enlists the aid of the women of Jerusalem.

> I adjure you, O daughters of Jerusalem,
>> if you find my lover, what should you say to him?
>> That I am sick with love! (5:8)

Being undeterred by the abuse of the guards, she continues to pursue the object of her desire by appealing to the daughters of Jerusalem for help. The daughters of Jerusalem, the chorus of the Song, serve many purposes throughout the book. They are her disciples in love, but here they will be her aid as she seeks love. As it turns out, she will not need them to find him, but she does not yet know that. So she gives them a message to relay to him, that she is lovesick. At the beginning of this poem, she had rebuffed him. He has left thinking she had no desire for intimacy, and now she desperately wants to get him the message that she yearns for his presence. She needs him, and her message is an exclamation of desire and a plea for union.

The women, surprisingly, are not easily recruited to the task. They answer the woman by asking,

> How is your lover better than (another) lover, O most beautiful of
>> women?
>> How is your lover better than (another) lover, that we should
>> so swear? (5:9)

Their reluctance is never explained, but it is clear what role their questions serve in the unfolding of the poem, since it provides the rationale for the woman to express her desire for the man by describing his beauty in the most erotic of terms. In other words, she answers their hesitation by describing the man.

> My lover is radiant and ruddy,
>> distinguished among ten thousand!
> His head is pure gold.
>> His locks are wavy, black like a raven.
> His eyes are like doves by water streams,
>> bathing in milk,
>> sitting by pools.
> His cheeks are like spice beds
>> growing aromatics.
> His lips are like lilies
>> dripping with liquid myrrh.
> His arms are bars of gold,
>> set with Tarshish-stones.
> His member is an ivory tusk,
>> ornamented with lapis.
> His legs are pillars of marble,
>> founded on gold pedestals.
> His appearance is like Lebanon,
>> choice like the cedars.
> His palate is sweet.
>> He is totally desirable.
> This is my lover and this is my darling, O daughters of Jerusalem.
>> (5:10–16)

Since we have treated this description in the chapter on beauty (see chap. 7), we refer to our comments there rather than provide interpretive detail again here, except to say that her description convinces the women of Jerusalem that this man is worth finding.

> Where did your lover go, O most beautiful of women?
>> Where did your lover turn,
>> that we may search for him with you? (6:1)

The woman's response to this question is unexpected, at least if we treat this poem like a straightforward story. She is looking for him and cannot find him; she has even enlisted the women to help her. But in response to their question, she has an answer.

> My lover went down to his garden,
>   to the bed of spices,
> to graze in the gardens,
>   to pluck the lilies.
> I belong to my lover,
>   and my lover belongs to me—
> he grazes among the lilies. (6:2–3)

He is in the garden. We must remember that the garden is the setting of intimacy between the man and the woman. Thus, her answer is not providing GPS directions to find him, but is an expression of her awareness that they will ultimately experience intimacy.

Thus this poem, which talks about the difficulties of experiencing the type of union that is often celebrated in the Song, ends with hope. But it is a story that recognizes the difficulty of intimate relationship. The man first approaches the woman asking her to open her door to him. She initially denies his overture, but soon is aroused herself. But when she eventually moves toward him, he is absent. Nevertheless, through the most difficult of conditions, she sets out to find him. The poem ends with the expectation of union.

This poem is not the only one in the Song that speaks of the struggle to achieve intimacy. Indeed, the poem that we read in 3:1–5 is similar in many ways to the one we just read. Again the woman is the speaker.

> On my bed at night I searched for the one my soul loves.
>   I searched for him, but I did not find him.
> "I will get up and go around in the city,
>   in the streets and the public areas.
> I will search for the one my soul loves."
>   I searched, but I did not find him.
> The guards found me, those who patrol the city.
>   "Have you seen the one my soul loves?"
> It was a little while after I left them that I found the one my soul
>   loves.
>   I grabbed him and would not let him go

until I brought him to my mother's house,
  to the room where she conceived me.
I adjure you, daughters of Jerusalem,
  by the gazelles or the deer of the field,
    not to awaken or arouse love until it desires.

The repetition of this motif in the Song is a way of indicating that struggle is not exceptional in an intimate relationship. Intimacy does not come easily. If the Song did not acknowledge this, then it would just be a type of romantic, utopian vision of relationship.

After all, any honest couple who has enjoyed a healthy relationship would share that that relationship does not always come naturally, but has been hard won through difficulties and disappointed expectations. The Song is about the redemption of sexuality, but this side of heaven it is always an already-but-not-yet redemption. Two redeemed sinners living in the intense crucible of a marriage relationship will not experience only unalloyed joy.

That is what is so tragic about marriages that fall apart because a spouse does not live up to the expectation that he or she will fulfill the other's needs. What is called for in such moments is not the pursuit of someone else but rather the pursuit of the relationship—to work for a union of heart, soul, and body. If the flame of love has diminished or gone out, then the response should be to work (and it is work) at rekindling affection and desire.

Passion is not meant to be the exception in a marriage; it is meant to be the norm.

Passion is not meant to be the exception in a marriage; it is meant to be the norm. When it is lost, it must be recovered, and it will only be regained by the hard, humbling labor to restore honor in lieu of overt or subtle violence and to restore intimacy instead of distance and disappointment. These poems point to the expectation that every marriage will have heartbreaking harm and disappointment and that all the labor to grow together is worth the cost. The struggle with sex also involves issues that arise from our family. We will address those realities in the next chapter.

13

The Struggle toward Intimacy

Part 2

Sexual intimacy and joy don't come easily for any couple. Seldom are desire, pleasure, or an orgasm equal in a single moment of love-making, let alone across the many seasons of a marriage. In the previous chapter, we considered obstacles to desire from outside the re-lationship. In this chapter we will consider poems that point to another potential impediment to the love between the man and the woman, and this potential obstacle comes from those who love us and care for us more than any other, or at least should—namely, our family. Further, our family and its expectations are shaped by a far more complex real-ity: culture. Both our family and culture need to be addressed in order to fully appreciate our struggle with sexual intimacy.

To understand the poems we will now examine, we have to understand how the ancient Israelite family is not exactly like our own (though views of the family that are similar to those of the ancient Israelites still exist today in some parts of the world). The social custom of the day dictated that a woman's brothers play a key role in the preparation of their sister for marriage. They, along with their father, were charged with protect-ing their sister from a man who would take advantage of her sexually before committing his life to caring for and protecting her. They were also involved in marriage negotiations on behalf of their sister. Such customs explain, for instance, the role of Dinah's brothers Levi and Simeon in Genesis 34.

With this background, we turn to Song of Songs 1:5–6 where the woman is speaking to the daughters of Jerusalem.

> I am dark, but beautiful, daughters of Jerusalem,
>> like the tents of Qedar,
>> like the curtains of Solomon.
> Don't look at me, because I am swarthy,
>> because the sun scorched me.
> My mother's sons were angry with me;
>> they made me guard vineyards,
>> but my vineyard I did not guard.

The woman's tone is defensive. She seems hurt, even apologetic for her appearance. The opening line ("I am dark, but beautiful") can appear controversial unless understood correctly. She is not talking about the natural color of her skin, which would have been dark since she is an Israelite woman. What she complains about is the effect of the sun on her complexion. It has further darkened her skin. The tents of Qedar, a nomadic people in Arabia, and of Solomon are used to give an impression of the climate-induced color of her skin.

Again, we must understand the woman's speech from the perspective of her culture. A deep tan is considered attractive in some cultures, but not hers. Manual labor is considered virtuous in many cultures, but not hers. And that is the point: her sun-darkened skin is the result of manual labor.

She defends herself against city girls, who would not be caught dead out in the fields working. Their skin, though naturally dark, would not be further darkened in a way that branded them as manual laborers.

But why is she working in the fields? Her brothers made her because they were angry at her. Notice, though, that she calls them not her brothers but rather her "mother's sons." That indirect way of referring to them is a way to distance herself from them and thus expresses her anger. It may also indicate that they are the agents of her parents. Her attitude likely indicates her belief that she is being treated unfairly.

And if she is being forced into physical labor in order to darken her skin to make her less attractive to possible suitors—and it certainly appears this is what is happening—then her brothers may be well intentioned in keeping her from promiscuity, but their harm is intrusive and disrespectful. She has more than legitimate reason to be furious.

Why are the brothers angry? The text does not say. From what we know about the brothers' role in protecting their sister's virtue before her marriage, maybe they think she is in jeopardy from either her own lust or another's. The woman, as we have already said, reacts not with guilt and confession but with irritation toward her brothers. Thus, we can fairly conclude that we are encouraged to think they have wronged her.

Most families are to some degree well-intentioned in their working to thwart the momentum of desire. But those efforts, even when they are the height of wisdom, often create unintended and heartbreaking consequences. Who knows with certainty either that a potential mate is the "right" choice or that the pairing is disastrous? We all know marriages that looked ideal at the start and then swerve to the disaster of divorce. And we know marriages that we would have bet strongly against that have grown and matured.

What is implied is not that families shouldn't get involved, but an approach of engagement and interaction is wildly different than one of intrusion and coercion. The end does not justify the means if harm is the result, even if unintended. The brothers in this scenario are simply wrong.

What is the significance of the vineyard? In a number of the poems we have already interpreted, we have seen that the vineyard (like the garden or the orchard or indeed the countryside) is the place of sexual intimacy. In other poems, it refers to the woman and her sexuality. Indeed, in this poem, the vineyard may have two nuances of meaning, and as we contemplate the vineyard, we must remember that we are dealing with a poem and not a literal, historical description of an event.

> What is implied is not that families shouldn't get involved, but an approach of engagement and interaction is wildly different than one of intrusion and coercion.

On the surface level, we are to think of the work that her brothers have put her to. She is engaged in physical labor with social consequences. Yet this suggests a more poetic reference to the vineyard, the woman's sexuality, perhaps in this case her physical desirability. The verse then indicates that her family was willing to darken her skin to taint her sexual appeal. The effect of this poem is to side with her against her family and also to affirm her assertiveness in the face of her domineering brothers.

Her assertiveness comes out even more strongly the second time the brothers make their appearance in the Song. Interestingly, and perhaps contributing to the cohesiveness of the book as a whole, while the first appearance is in the first chapter of the book, the second and final appearance is in the last. Here, though, the brothers actually speak.

> Our sister is small,
>   and she has no breasts.
> What should we do for our sister
>   on the day she is spoken for?
> If she is a wall, we will build a silver battlement for her.
>   But if she is a door, we will enclose her with a cedar board.
>   (8:8–9)

The brothers' speech indicates that brothers are responsible for their sister in preparation for marriage. They show their concern for her, but speak as if she is immature, indicated by her small breasts, and not yet ready for marriage.

We must remember that the typical marriage age today (and for the past hundred or more years) is much older than in antiquity. Today the average marriage age of a woman is about twenty-seven. During the time period of the Old Testament, it would not have been unusual at all for a woman to be married right after she became sexually mature, at age thirteen or soon after. Men would not have been much older. The delay in marriage age was occasioned by the move from an agrarian culture to an industrial one, as well as the introduction of widespread education that prolongs adolescence and delays economic independence into the twenties. What this means is that today, in contrast to antiquity, men and women are married an average of ten or more years after they become sexually interested, putting incredible pressure on young people when they are at their most virile. We will return to this subject later.

As we said, the brothers operate as if they want the best for their sister, yet they fail to care for her. They want to know what they should do to prepare her for her marriage day ("the day she is spoken for"). Interestingly, they answer their own question, but their answer may strike many as opaque since they use metaphorical language.

What does it mean to say that she is a wall? Or that she is a door?

The difference between a wall and a door is that the latter is penetrable. In terms of the woman, if she is door-like, then she is promiscuous or at least open to having sex. This interpretation is confirmed by our analysis of the poem in 5:2–6:3, which opens with the man at the door asking the woman to open up to him. If door points to promiscuity, then wall means she has not opened herself up to other men.

Thus, the brothers plot their strategy to protect their sister based on her character. If she is a wall (that is, not penetrated or penetrable), they will build a silver battlement on the wall. A battlement is a fortification of a wall where soldiers can gather and repel any attackers. In other words, the brothers say they will come alongside their sister and support her in her determination to remain chaste until marriage. Of course, real battlements were not built of silver. Poetically, the precious metal indicates that the brothers will honor their sister for her intent to save herself for her marriage day.

That said, the brothers imagine a second scenario—that their sister is a door. If she is promiscuous, they will put an end to that by placing a cedar board over her door. Cedar is not only a fragrant and precious board; it is also hard.

The brothers have prepared their strategy, but their sister quickly responds.

> I am a wall, and my breasts are like towers.
> Thus, I will be in his eyes like one who brings peace. (8:10)

The brothers may be well intentioned, but they are clueless, and their suspicion is unfounded. First, their worries are unfounded because the woman is a wall. She has determined to save herself for her marriage day. They are clueless because, far from being immature ("she has no breasts"), she is mature ("my breasts are like towers"). Likely this statement is operating on two levels: The brothers are clueless because they have not noticed their sister's body has matured. And equally, the brothers are clueless because they have failed to read the character of their sister. Tragically, it is often still the case that more effort is put toward defending virginity than nurturing a love for pleasure and honor.

They are interacting with her as if she is promiscuous. Instead, she is sensual, aroused, and arousing while also being committed to honoring her body and the healthy expectations of her culture. She is both erotic and a woman of peace.

Thus, she will be in her eventual husband's eyes as one who brings "peace." The Hebrew word for peace is the well-known *shalom*, which can mean harmony, and is the state of the human condition before the introduction of sin. In Eden, there was *shalom* between God and humans, and thus between humans.

In the Song, the man and the woman are anonymous. They are general types, not specific individuals. Thus, as described in the first chapter, every married couple can identify with the man and the woman. But there is one male name found in the Song: Solomon (*Shelomo* in Hebrew). And once (6:13) the woman is called the Shulammite. As we have seen before, it is not coincidental that both names are derived from the Hebrew word *shalom*. In other words, when Shelomo and Shulammite come together, what is the result? Super *shalom*.

The brothers' role in these two poems is first of all a reminder that family plays a critical role in our sexual development. The focus on the woman, not the man, should not let us lose sight that the same is true for both of them, though it is the father who would have had a direct role in instructing his son to avoid illicit sexual relationships (see Prov. 5–7). The biblical witness is united with the Song of Songs in encouraging both women and men to save the intimacy of sexual intercourse for the deep emotional and covenantal commitment of marriage.

This biblical concern is not a matter of killing pleasure. It is not an expression of "if it feels good, it must be wrong." Far from it. What God wants is for a man and a woman to be intimate allies without shame. Remember Adam and Eve naked in the Garden of Eden.

But why the need for protection, particularly for the woman? Let's first consider this question from the perspective of the biblical period. An unmarried woman was extremely vulnerable in ancient Israel; one only has to read the book of Ruth to understand this.

The reality was that the same was not true for a man. After all, a man in the ancient world (and, for that matter, a modern man) can have a sexual relationship with minimal consequences. In a word, men don't get pregnant. Thus, the protections around a woman in the Bible are a matter of justice. A woman could not just be used and cast aside. God does not want women to be exploited by men. He wants men and women to enjoy an intimate relationship protected by commitment.

Of course, the modern world is not exactly like the ancient world. Women may still be fighting for equality, but they are far, far from being as vulnerable as they were in the ancient world. Women, in short, can take care of themselves, at least in the West. In other more familial cultures where independence is often frowned upon, it is a different and evolving story. In the West it is far more the case that women don't need men in order to make their way in the world.

In response, we first point out something that many Western people forget, which is that in the vast majority of the world, a woman needs protection as much as a woman in the ancient world did. The data is staggering regarding the amount of sexual and physical harm against women that occurs with little judicial or familial intervention. Many books, such as *Half the Sky*,[1] and many documentaries have exposed the relentless and dark harm many women in both Western and non-Western countries suffer as a matter of course.

In the West, where women can make it economically on their own as well as men can, the level of intimacy, not only physical but also emotional, psychological, and spiritual, that is expressed in sexual intercourse is such that it must be protected by a public and legal commitment, what the Bible calls a covenant.

That said, we feel it foolish to think that outside of marriage there should be no physical intimacy between a man and a woman. In answer to how far is too far, we have heard those who teach that even kissing and intimate touching should be reserved for marriage. Such a view is unrealistic and even absurd and puts unbelievable pressures on young single people, particularly in modern times, when marriage tends to be delayed till long after the point of sexual maturation.

Perhaps the best principle, though it is not a law, is that the level of intimacy should not exceed the level of commitment that a man and a woman have for each other. A couple that is engaged have entered a level of commitment that is far beyond that of a couple in their first month of dating, but still short of the full-blown commitment of marriage. Physical intimacy should not exceed the level of commitment that a couple have for each other.

Thus, in many ways, the answer to how far is too far is a matter not of law but of wisdom, guided by the principle that the deeper a couple's commitment to one other, the more physically intimate they will be. However, as in all matters of wisdom, it is a question not only of timing but also of knowing oneself. It's like drinking alcohol. Some people can have a drink and enjoy God's gift of wine (Ps. 104:15), but others will have a drink and not be able to stop until they are passed-out drunk. Again, a committed couple needs to know each other and talk to each other about their relationship and what makes them feel safe. Having wisdom, not law, as pivotal in navigating an intimate relationship can itself be a frightening prospect. Having a law ("no kissing until engagement") is so much easier and more clear-cut, but the Bible does not give us a law, short of reserving sexual intercourse for marriage. Though easier and more clear-cut, to have laws ruling physical intimacy in a relationship of love would also be legalistic and unrealistic. An unrealistic law is not a law that is likely to be obeyed.

But how do we grow in wisdom? The first answer to that question is that we develop a vibrant relationship with Jesus, who is the very epitome of God's wisdom (Col. 2:2–3). The Old Testament describes wisdom as a relationship with a woman named Wisdom (Prov. 8:1–9:6), who represents God himself.[2] The bottom line, for the Old and the New Testaments, is that wisdom fundamentally involves a relationship with God ("the fear of the LORD is the beginning of knowledge," Prov. 1:7 NIV).

Someone who has a healthy relationship with God would be heartbroken at the thought of exploiting another person sexually. Rather they will relate to that person sexually in a way that deepens their relationship on an emotional, psychological, and spiritual level. When sex is used merely as a form of pleasure, like drinking a beer, it inevitably becomes a commodity to be used by both parties and is trivialized. If sex is being used to supercharge the momentum of intimacy, then the speed attained will outrun the solidity of the relationship, and as a result the character of the relationship will fail to grow as God intended. Too many relationships that begin and progress through sex fail to grow the true skills needed for intimacy because they achieved a level of closeness through sex that will not last when the struggles of sexuality increase or when sexual drives lessen.

> Someone who has a healthy relationship with God would be heartbroken at the thought of exploiting another person sexually.

The book of Proverbs not only informs us of the starting point and foundation of wisdom in our relationship with God, but also encourages us to grow in wisdom by listening to others who are more mature than we are. We also learn through our experiences and observations of life. Further—and this is the hardest, most frightening avenue of wisdom—we learn through our mistakes.

And have no doubt about it, living by wisdom is difficult. There will be failure. We will make mistakes by hurting others and by being hurt by others, and we should grieve those failures and seek forgiveness. But the solution is not to live by a series of human-made rules that sap all vitality out of the life and love that God has given us to enjoy.

In her response to her brothers, the woman indicates that the time has come for her to break away from their control and protection. The brothers, representing the appropriate concern of the family to help their sister guard her sexuality before marriage, seem to have overplayed their hand in the poems of the Song. In a word, there comes a time to "leave" family and be united with one's spouse, including physically (see Gen. 2:24 and Ps. 45:10).

Leaving is a process that begins well before the marriage ceremony. In some ways it begins as children learn to own and play with their bodies. All children will need to understand that their bodies are their own, to be honored and cared for as gifts from God. And the only way that can be done is through experimentation and play. Just as children can't learn to relate to others without play, so children can't play without testing their bodies in relation with the bodies of others. The simple recess game of four square is an exercise in hand-eye coordination, rule keeping, sharing responsibility, waiting your turn, and living with the reality that some bodies are faster, quicker, and more adept at the game than others.

Leaving involves letting go of one world to embrace a new realm. There is both loss and gain in leaving, and we prepare children for losses and successes through play. Why would we assume it would be any different with regard to our sexuality? Many naively assume that we become sexual as adolescents and that the great concern is to escape bad decisions, remain chaste, and learn how to wait for the right time and person.

The Song of Songs explores the tension of this even when the bride was likely to be married at a near prepubescent age. The choice to remain chaste doesn't remove the struggle or the inevitable complexities of what our families will do with our sexuality. In fact, it guarantees that sexuality is going to be made far more complex by our family story.

Let us restate the complexity. If you let children/adolescents wander into their sexuality with no input, then you turn them over to their peers and the powers of the marketing culture that uses sex more frequently than any other desire or motive. If you choose to get involved, then you may bumble and abuse as foolishly as the "brothers." Families should be involved with their children's sexual development, but only with a spirit of humility and wisdom, asking for a great deal of grace. A child/adolescent cannot learn to masturbate, flirt, develop desire, grow to discern character in another, or mature at all without the possibility of failure. If we expect our children eventually to leave well, then we have to develop a way of making sexual failure not the catastrophic apocalypse that it often becomes in many conservative homes.

As well, there has to be more nuanced—not merely awkward—conversation about what it means to explore, play, experiment, and fundamentally own our bodies with pleasure, joy, and honor for ourselves and others. The Song sings to the high call of pleasure and joy without denying the complexities or heartache.

14

After the
Bible Study on Struggles

haven't done this often, but I reread my last couple of entries. I am not a fan of sentimentality and I fear what I wrote is dripping with wistfulness. I actually felt repulsed with my maudlin meanderings about Jon and Celeste and then had to wipe away the tears. Of all things, tears. It wasn't allergies, and if it was what I supposedly fear—sentimentality—then why did the tears feel good? More than good, why did they feel right? Alive even? I am near another conversion and not sure I want the weight (or is it the freedom?) it might provide.

I have said yes to Jesus, but so far I have not spoken any real no's that impede or alter my life. There is something in me that is different, and what seems to be growing is the capacity to believe that life is better than it appears, or that maybe there is an author of life who is better than he appears. But there is this vexing struggle with sex. And given that these poems are all about sex, then I must follow the track they are inviting me to consider. The goodness of this God who has authored sexuality seems starkly in contrast with the cruelty that spins around the supposed goodness of sex.

Yesterday a customer told me that I was "f—ing nuts and if you think I can't get a better deal you can go f— yourself." I can't be the only one alive who has figured out that the most used f-word on the books is mostly used as a violent curse, the wish for your degradation. I tossed away his curse as if it were paper, but it lingered like a sulfurous cloud over my day. I backpedaled and apologized for insulting him and agreed to rewrite the deal. I was in his office for the day, so I altered paragraphs and lowered the price, while increasing the down payment and the terms of financing so he was going to lose more money over the life of the loan. Then I threw in season tickets to the Braves, a case of Moose Drool, and ten boxes of 9-millimeter shells. He ended up smiling like a Buddha.

Screw or be screwed. Survival of the horniest, who gets the top position. It is all so basic. I feel constantly on the edge of cynical use or indulged dissipation. And I am not sure what to do with this. What I am choosing at the moment is not to abort the nascent hope. It may be fleeting, but there is no need at this instant to send it prematurely into exile.

I always thought sex was a way of escaping life; instead I am finding that sex is a lens through which to assess every portion of my life. One thing that is occurring through this Bible study is that I am thinking more about sex than I ever have. I thought I thought about sex a lot, but now it seems like I take a mystery tour through my lovers and loves as if I am a tourist on a bus to hell, or maybe on a trip to Bountiful.

As I wind my way through the murky memories, I remember mostly drama or boredom. In every new relationship there was a period of excitement and novelty where discovering the idiosyncrasies of the body and mind of my partner brought a chemical high. I could taste the rush of anticipation like what a gambler must feel when he turns into the casino parking lot. Alive. Electric lady land. The process always felt taboo and free from the eventual hurt and disappointment that occludes all sex. But hurt always comes, disappointment grows like weeds in an expert gardener's yard. No matter how much you know or care, weeds mar the verdant green like graffiti on train cars. Each car bears the tag of some nascent artist whose mark is self-aggrandizing. Each disappointment is distinct, but after a while it all blends into a boring sameness. The drama of a new relationship moves from enchantment and excitement to petty disappointments and differences, then continues with loss, pursuit, and return, until you start over, collect your two hundred dollars for passing "Go," and hope you don't land in jail this time around.

The relationship that just ended a few weeks ago needed to die a far faster death. I let it go on for almost a year, on and off, in a form of mutual tarring and feathering. Joselyn loved shoes and flirting to try to get self-serve gas station owners to fill her tank, and she dreamed of someday making it onto a reality television show. She also read about epistemology and worked out regularly on a climbing wall. My generation loves irreconcilable disjunctions, and she was the queen of elegant contradictions.

It ended with a text.

The log cabin quilt
tossed on the floor
covers only one

Our threads unravel
masked by drama
hides only one

Lies collect like leaves
littered copse
alone I rake.

Good-bye Malcolm

I tried to call. For a week. Each time I pulled up her name I always wondered what I would say. "I'm sorry." Or, "Why end it in such a cowardly way through a text?" "Do you still want to hang out?" "You still have my Amherst sweatshirt—it was a gift from another woman who dumped me, and pretty nostalgic. Can I get it back?" It all felt so pointless.

Still, I mostly feel relieved. The relationship was about getting enough adrenaline to mask the boredom with flits of drama. Part of our problem was that neither of us had any standard boundaries that could easily be flaunted to raise the drama quotient, so our drama had to come solely from conflict. We fought, fled, hid, slithered back, kissed, and slid back to the same conflict. Sex simply seemed like a migration from exile to a temporary shelter, only to discover you were more alone in your adopted home than you'd been when you were an exile dreaming of a new world.

I have seen the same insanity with more stability with Marty and Jill. Their mutual affair ended Marty's last marriage and brought them into their current marital bliss. She flirts for what they can never have and satisfies the craving instead with self-righteousness. She is the one person in the room most likely never to stray, solely due to the pride of her resolve. If that is love, then I don't see any reason to lay my five cards down and ask for an entirely new hand.

Then there is Lois. She is a neon-light ad for singleness. She is a mess, but oddly lovable. Or maybe she is more lovable because she is a mess. Who knows? All I know is she got the dirt beat into her by a man who is part of a Christian cult that practices domestic discipline on their wives. I thought I was sexually deviant, but these dudes are recklessly self-righteous beyond comprehension, to the point of having actual websites that talk about whether it is better to spank with pants on, only underwear, or bare butt. The benefit of bare, they say, is that one can tell when bruising may occur—but one idiot writes that it is also possible to be aroused when spanking with bare buttocks and thus confound the discipline with arousal.

Oh my, the Marquis de Sade thought those thoughts well before these men. To think that this form of sadomasochism is blessed by biblical writ makes me quake. Truly there are so many loony-tune beliefsheviks that to say I am a Christian means to cohabit with some of the best and worst people on the earth.

The one who is most difficult for me to comprehend is Amihan. She grew up in a Christian home where she heard at a precocious age that she was a lovely and desirable apple. But every time she wore clothing that caused a man to lust she became less pure and desirable. If she let a boy touch her, she was letting the apple be marred. If she had had sex, even if it was not terribly well defined, she was letting some goober take a bite out of her, and the apple would get dark and uneatable. Of course, the same litany was never said to the boys, but alas, why worry about gender equality?

My path was license. Her path was litigious. I wanted boundaries and lived with the burden of figuring out what was good to eat from this bounty of pleasure; Amihan didn't want license, just freedom from the court of accusation when and if her experimentation took some tough turns.

She is the most honest regarding her sexual struggles and, other than Jon and Celeste, the most holy. She has been judged as a bad apple and celebrated as a virgin—yet she grieves never having had intercourse. She remains a conundrum on the side of both struggle and choice.

Choose your poison: Sex is the cure. Sex is the disease. Sex is never just sex. If I have learned anything so far, it is that it is naive to think that anyone escapes the heartache and hope of becoming a sexual being and sexually being with someone else.

I heard Jon talk about this next section of poems as a reflection on the glory of sex, love, and marriage—the whole enchilada. I can see why this entire following Jesus thing requires faith. If I look at all that is in front of me and what is available, I find no more glory in it than the Rose Bowl parade. It is an extravaganza that only looks good as long as you observe it far, far away in television land. To get close up is to be easily lost in the flower petals and the hubris of what it takes to make a float. But if I listen for long to the ache in me for something that lasts and that satisfies, then I have bought into a nostalgia that lingers like the longing to return to childhood. Given that my childhood was not a piece of cake, I can only wonder what is the glory I am supposed to see or at least dream.

P.S. (two days later) I don't like the feeling of being set up. On one hand, it feels like being a pawn under the control of an all-knowing chess player. On the other, I know I am being moved and can feel the energy of the transition but am not sure of either the point or the outcome. I know I am being played with, and it simply doesn't feel good, or bad. Obviously, I want to know the genius behind the move and the outcome of the turn. And I am not given access to know beyond this simple knowing.

Okay, the set-up: I am listening to Natalie Merchant. Why? Because it is in my iTunes and it just showed up, sort of. I had it on random, and she barges into my run, singing as if she is an older man who just lost his wife. The ache in her voice and the rumination on how life will be lived without his wife is more than I can bear.

Tears again. Four miles into a run—deep into the woods, up and down, steady, solid, smelling the decaying fragrances of the forest in transition from autumn to early, early winter—and Natalie decides to remind me that I have lost love without ever having the benefit of loving. Sucks.

And if this is not bad enough, the next day, with Natalie long forgotten, I watch an older couple cross the street while I wait in my car at a stoplight. She is scarecrow thin, dressed in a below-the-knee knitted dress, a tightly enclosed jacket with the button at the neck closed to the world, her purple scarf elegantly tied in the fashion that only the French seem to comprehend. Beside her, her husband holds onto her arm, slightly stooped, looking well worn in a tweed jacket and dark gray pants. His shoes sparkle with a new shine.

The light turned and they walked across the street at a pace the city fathers had not timed the lights to honor. It was a slow, labored progress that seemed glacial. They were halfway across when the light turned again. I watched the car in the other lane lurch forward and honk. I felt rage, protective fury. I couldn't believe some idiot would interrupt the stage of this regal couple with the whiny irritation of a Toyota horn.

I expected her to turn her formidable severity toward the crud. Instead, she gripped the man's arm with a slight, confirming touch and ignored the interruption. They arrived at their curb with tenderness and honor. The Toyota honked again for good measure and wheeled away in indignant disgust. Idiot.

I drove on cursing the fool until I realized that I had missed the drama being played out for me. Of course Natalie showed up in lilting reminder that what I had witnessed is far from my grasp. I have no one to help me navigate the streets of life, let alone do so with such dignity and care. I am a pawn, when I think I am a king. Seems like it is time to start thinking about death.

15

Before the
Bible Study on Glory

read the glory material this week prior to the gathering. Usually I read what I need to digest in the way I eat a hot dog. No need for delicacy or fine bone china—just slam it down with a lot of relish and forget what you have just eaten. I take the Bible in the same way. I know it is the Word, God's inspired, inerrant, and indelicate Word, but I prefer to snack on truth rather than have it as a five-course meal. So I cram as much as I can, as close to the time of the Bible study as possible, and pretend to be far more prepared than I am. This time is different. I ate the Word slowly and chewed the requisite fifty times before swallowing; I didn't want to choke to death. I also didn't want to miss a wisp or nuance of what was being said.

Solomon's wedding was over the top. A bit of grandiosity and military pomp. Not sure why the dude has to have battle-weary soldiers waltz him to the front of the church, but maybe that is what the silly dudes in tuxedos are meant to represent when they stand with the groom—a frilly military guard. But as I have been thinking about what it means to get married and the struggles it brings, maybe the guards are there as much to make sure the groom doesn't bolt as they are there to witness and protect.

To wed your beloved and to bind your heart to a woman is more than I have allowed myself to consider. I know it terrifies me, especially when I look at my father's infidelities, my mom's efforts to suck me dry, and then add a divorce rate that is not much of a promise of a life of bliss.

Again, I know I am on the cusp of conversion—either the pomp and splendor is like a fog that hides, if not causes, the sixty-car pileup ahead or it is a symbol of the cloud of glory that is supposed to lead those desert wanderers into their promised home. I feel split. What I see around me says the pomp is a grandiose fog, an illusion, a gambit to prove our families are rich and we have a foot up on all those around us. But then I look even at the marriage of Marty and Jill, and as crazy as they are, there is still something good between them. She is a dry drunk; he is always on the edge of flirtatious narcissism—but they have weathered affairs, heartache, and trauma, and they remain together.

Even as I look at train-wreck Lois, I can't deny that she is an odd and brave woman. She has not fled the hard and sensual discussions on sex even when I thought she might actually vomit venom during our discussions. It may be obvious, but I like her gutsy, take-no-prisoners approach to her husband's abuse. She has turned out to be a fighter and more tender than I would have ever, ever imagined when we began. Okay, I like these people and I respect everyone's heart, and oddly, in honoring their sexual struggles I have come to my own war with a little more—okay, maybe not a huge amount, but a little more—kindness.

I can't deny what I see in the world: marriages are a mess. But I also can't deny that I like the integrity of these broken men and women. What I am haunted by is not the opulence but the ferocity of what I perceive to be the love of this couple in the Song. I have to write it out just to read it again word for word.

Set me like a seal on your heart,
like a seal on your arm.
For love is as strong as Death;
passion is as tenacious as the Grave.

Its flame is an intense fire,
    a god-like flame.
Many waters are not able to extinguish love,
    nor rivers flood it.
Even if a person gave all the wealth of his house for love,
    he would be completely despised. (8:6–7)

My struggle with, hatred for, and love of sex is really a war with endings, loss, and desire. In some ways, the end returns to the beginning. The sexual battle is really a war with desire. If I let myself name the amount of sexual harm done to me and perpetrated by me against others, it raises the question, will I ever know what it means to feel innocent and free? Will I ever be free of death?

Here we go again. On one hand, death will unquestionably take me and the one I love. I almost can't bear the thought that not only is sex central to my war with shame, but it is also going to increase my grief when it ends if I were to ever allow my heart truly to love.

And then, the audacity of this poetic claim—that love is as strong as death, a god-like flame, and many waters can't drown it, that sexual passion rises and falls like a gasoline fire—it is hot, intense, quick and then gone, glorious but ephemeral. But the residue of that sexual passion is part of a deeper, white-hot, god-like fire that taunts death with a tattoo.

I want to scream my bloody head off. I have been marked by an older teenager in Florida, my teacher in eighth grade, my mother, and all the fantasies they have engendered through memory-fueled masturbation, pornography, and sex. Marked. I have had my body possessed and owned by people who were sexual marauders simply passing through the neighborhood with no desire or plan to stay. I became as much a perpetrator as those who harmed me.

And now this poem tells me that I was meant to take on the seal of another, burn their love into my heart and arm, and rise as a warrior, axis bold as love, weapon in hand, eyes afire, and plunge the dagger into the heart of death and say, "I'll die with her name on my lips." She will die looking into my eyes, thanking me for all the days we lived together in delight and passion.

131

It is too much. I can't keep writing. If I say the words, I can't remain the same. If I confess that this is what I want and dream that one day it might be mine, then what do I do with the ruins behind me or the vast desert of uncertainty that is ahead? Doubt has been my comfort, and cynicism has been my meat. To trust and obey, to trust goodness feels so foolish, and to obey desire, to actually enter the holy ground of what I truly desire is to obey my heart in a way that feels far scarier than merely dying.

Do I want to sit at the bed of the woman I have loved for fifty years and speak the absurdly simple and ineloquent words "thank you"? And do so as a testament, a witness that abuse, shame, heartache, frustration, and failure didn't win?

I do.

If no one can escape the mark of sexuality in this life, then I want to bear the seal that mocks all the harm I have known. I think I am ready to say what I have been unwilling to say through these meandering writings.

I will trust love. I will give myself to lovemaking that only burnishes the seal on my arm. I believe love will vanquish all heartache, harm, and death.

16

The Glory of Sex

We have seen the dangers and risks of physical intimacy. Indeed, we have seen enough that we might want to do everything we can to avoid being ensnared in such a complex and risky relationship. It might bring more harm than good. No wonder that after the introduction of sin into the world, Adam and Eve immediately covered their nakedness and then ran for cover!

However, the earlier chapters of this book examined songs that celebrate desire and beauty and describe sexual scenes that urge us to take the risk. Now we will look at a poem that announces the grandeur of committed relationship and love as it describes a royal wedding procession.

> THE WOMAN
> What is this coming up from the wilderness
>   like a pillar of smoke,
>   perfumed with myrrh and frankincense,
>   from all the scented powders of the trader?
> Look sharp, it is the palanquin of Solomon;
>   sixty heroes surround it,
>   Israel's heroes.
> All of them bear the sword;
>   they are battle-trained.

Each one has his sword on his thigh,
    against the terrors of the night.
The king has made a litter for himself;
    that is, Solomon—from the wood of Lebanon.
Its posts he made of silver;
    its canopy of gold;
its riding seat of purple;
    its interior inlaid with love by the daughters of Jerusalem.
Come and look, O daughters of Zion,
    at King Solomon with the crown with which his mother
    crowned him,
on the day of his wedding,
    on the day of his heart's joy! (3:6–11)

This poem highlights the glory of marriage by describing the magnificent spectacle of a royal wedding. It is clearly Solomon's wedding, but it is not a historical report of an actual wedding.

Indeed, the choice of Solomon as the groom is an interesting one since, according to the historical books (particularly 1 Kings 11), Solomon was anything but a model of love and marriage. After all, "he had seven hundred wives of royal birth and three hundred concubines, and his wives led him astray" (1 Kings 11:3 NIV). It is likely that Solomon's wedding was chosen for description because of its opulence.

Why opulence? Opulence is an external means to highlight the grandeur of the institution of marriage. Not everyone can or should have an opulent wedding. In fact, many people pour more money into a wedding than they or their families can possibly afford. In the United States in 2014, the average wedding costs over $28,000. In whatever way the day is marked, it is meant to be different from every other day before and after.

> As instituted in the Garden of Eden, marriage is the only human relationship that is strictly exclusive.

It is, after all, a very special day, honoring the start of a unique relationship. And here we use "unique" in its intended meaning rather than as hyperbole; there is no other human relationship like it. As instituted in the Garden of Eden, marriage is the only human relationship that is strictly exclusive. Marriage is a relationship of one man and one woman. No other human relationship allows for only one person.

With this as a background to the poem in 3:6–11, let's now explore some of the details.

The poem begins with a question. The woman sees a pillar of smoke in the wilderness and asks about its source. The pillar of smoke is seen not with the eyes but with the poetic imagination, because, though it is at a distance, she also smells its sweet fragrance. When reading of the pillar of smoke in the wilderness, the sensitive reader of the Old Testament will think of the pillar of smoke in the wilderness that accompanied the Israelites as they journeyed from Egypt to the promised land (Exod. 13:20–22). And indeed, our subtle poet likely intends us to make that connection as an allusion to the presence of God at this wedding party.

All of a sudden the cause of the pillar of smoke becomes clear. It is the palanquin of Solomon. A palanquin is a litter on which the occupant reclines, carried, in this case, by men, and surrounded by sixty battle-trained warriors. Thus, the palanquin is a symbol not only of wealth and luxury but also of power.

But why is Solomon accompanied by soldiers at his wedding? Is it simply an honor guard? It is that, but likely more. These armed and battle-scarred men are ready to take on any threats ("the terrors of the night") that might come upon the bride and the groom. It is as if the bride and groom will be taken from the wedding in an antique Rolls Royce that is surrounded by a heavily armed Seal Team Six honor guard.

But what is being said?

We saw earlier how the Song addresses the risks and threats of the intimate relationship between a man and a woman in love. These threats are not specifically identified because they can come in many different forms, but ultimately every threat emanates from spiritual enemies.

Indeed, the spiritual nature of the threats may not have been far from our Old Testament poet's mind. After all, in the intertestamental book called Tobit, found in the Apocrypha, the night threats are demons who attack newly married couples on their wedding night. As Marvin Pope described it, these demons "were believed to be especially dangerous at nuptial affairs and to lie in wait for newlyweds."[1]

The New Testament reminds the Christian that we are engaged in a spiritual battle and that behind our human challenges and struggles lies a spiritual battle against the "rulers, against the authorities, against the powers of this dark world and against the spiritual forces of evil in the heavenly realms" (Eph. 6:12 NIV).

Granted, Paul is not speaking specifically of marriage here, but if God loves sex and marriage, then the devil hates it and will work to its destruction from day one. But Christians have every reason to put their trust in God and to "put on the full armor of God, so that when the day of evil comes, you may be able to stand your ground, and after you have done everything, to stand" (Eph. 6:13 NIV).

Verses 8 and 9 return to the opulence and beauty of the palanquin. Notice the description of its parts. It is made from the wood of Lebanon. The wood of Lebanon simply was the best lumber at the time. As such, it was relatively rare and expensive, and thus it is an indication of wealth. It was used in the temple and the royal palace, for instance. During Solomon's lifetime, he imported it through the agency of the wealthy city of Tyre, north of Israel.

The passage goes on to describe its posts, canopy, riding seat, and interior. Though the specific details are hard to pin down, the main point is clear. The overall impression of the description of the palanquin emphasizes its luxury. It radiates wealth and power. It is constructed from the most precious of materials: silver, gold, and purple cloth, all associated with royalty. Purple cloth was particularly rare and expensive, made from a pigment from the Murex shellfish.

Such magnificence is not an end in itself. Rather it emphasizes the glory of love, and even more specifically the grandeur of marriage that creates the context for the ultimate expression of love between two human beings.

Indeed, the grandeur leads to rapture, as when the woman now exhorts the daughters of Zion (elsewhere referred to as "the daughters/women of Jerusalem") to take it all in ("come and look," v. 11). Marriage is not a private affair, but a public proclamation that invites others to witness and celebrate. We participate in the glory of the wedding of others.

In particular, the woman invites the daughters to look specifically at the groom's wedding crown, the one with which his mother crowned her son on the day of his marriage. Though this almost certainly describes an ancient Israelite wedding custom (which was likely not just reserved for the king), we have no other sources of information about it. A groom was likely crowned (not with an ornate crown, but perhaps with a simple garland) that indicated that this was his special day, a day like no other.

Thus, this poem highlights the glory of marriage as the epitome of love through a description of the grandeur of a royal wedding. It invites the daughters of Zion to relish and participate in the joy. However, other passages in the Song serve to warn them (and through them, us) to be careful not to quickly jump into such a wonderfully enjoyable yet complex relationship.

These passages are not whole poems, but rather a refrain that recurs (with some variation) three times in the Song at the culmination of an individual song. They are exhortations of the woman to the daughters of Jerusalem, and the repetition helps give the book, which we have seen is composed of separate love poems, a sense of cohesion.

The first occurrence of the refrain comes at the end of the poem found in 2:1–7, which we treated in detail in chapter 10 ("The Fantasy of Sexual Play"). We saw that it is a particularly passionate interchange between the man and the woman as they compliment each other's beauty and attest to their desire for each other. Their lovemaking is pleasant yet exhausting, so the woman requests sustenance to energize her for more. Her final words, though, are for the daughters who are her disciples in love.

> I adjure you, daughters of Jerusalem,
>> by the gazelles or the deer of the field,
>> not to awaken or arouse love until it desires. (2:7)

The woman speaks these words again to the daughters at the end of the song found in 3:1–5, which we briefly explored in chapter 12, on sexual struggles. In this poem sexual intimacy does not come easily, but when it does arrive, it comes with overwhelming force.

> I grabbed him and would not let him go
> until I brought him to my mother's house,
>> to the room where she conceived me. (3:4)

In the aftermath of her passion, she turns to the daughters and says,

> I adjure you, daughters of Jerusalem,
>> by the gazelles or the deer of the field,
>>> not to awaken or arouse love until it desires. (3:5)

The third occurrence of the refrain appears at the end of a poem that we have not yet considered, which is spoken by the woman and begins,

> Oh, that you were like my brother,
>> who sucked at the breasts of my mother!
> Then I would find you in public and kiss you,
>> and they would not shame me.
> I would lead you; I would bring you
>> to the house of my mother who taught me.
> I would make you drink spiced wine,
>> from my own pomegranate wine.
> His left hand is under my head,
>> and his right embraces me. (8:1–3)

The sentiment expressed by the woman at the start of the poem strikes us as strange since we are distanced from the cultural context in which the poem was written. Cultures have different standards for the public display of emotions. Many Americans, for instance, find it strange that men in Arab cultures will hold hands in public, while some of those same cultures find the public embrace of a man and woman off-putting.

Reading between the lines, it appears that the Israelite culture in which this poem was written found the public display of affection acceptable when it was between siblings but not when it was between a husband and a wife. After all, the latter has erotic overtones lacking in the former. The woman, though, wishes that she could enjoy in public the physical pleasures with the man that would lead to the more intimate pleasures of the bedroom.

As she imagines and fantasizes about those pleasures, she again, for the third and last time, turns to the daughters to instruct them.

> I adjure you, daughters of Jerusalem,
>> do not awaken and do not arouse love until it desires. (8:4)

The thrice-repeated refrain signals to the reader of the Song that the woman imparts an important message not only for the daughters but also for the readers of the Song—that is, for us even today in the twenty-first century. That message, in short, is that timing is everything (again a matter of wisdom [see chap. 13]).

First note that she speaks to the daughters with urgency ("I adjure you, daughters of Jerusalem"). It is crucial that they hear and respond to her. Indeed, she backs up her plea with a call that they take an oath (missing from the third occurrence of the formula), and a rather strange one, "by the gazelles and the deer of the field." Typically, an Israelite would swear by God, not by gazelles and deer.

However, the reader of the English Bible misses a subtle allusion to God that is found in the Hebrew original. The Song's oath formula is *bisba'ot 'o be'aylot hassadeh*, which sounds similar to "by the (LORD) of Hosts or by God Almighty" (*be[YHWH] seba'ot 'o be'el saddai*). In short, the poet is being playful here, implicitly pointing to a divine oath while not explicitly mentioning God. Or to put it another way, though God is not mentioned explicitly (here or anywhere in the Song of Songs), he is subtly present in the background.

But to what is it that she wants them to swear? "Not to arouse or to awaken love until it so desires." That is, she does not want the daughters, her disciples, to impulsively rush into a relationship like the one that she has with the man.

But why? She certainly seems to be enjoying herself, and the Song sings the praises of physical intimacy. Why shouldn't she want them to join her in joy?

She worries that the daughters will enter such an intense and risky relationship too quickly. Love is hard work and risky. They need to wait for the right time and the right person.

Interestingly, her instruction is serious, yet given playfully. She is not heavy handed; indeed, the warning itself is titillating. She is not asking these single women to repress any desire, but is asking them not to fan its flames until the right time. Christians sometimes misread Jesus's admonition not to lust (Matt. 5:27–30) as an admonition to stifle all desire, but lust is different from desire. Lust is an energy to possess and use, not one that attracts a man to a woman or a woman to a man.[2] To tell singles not to desire sex or to forbid the poetic anticipation of it before marriage is to ask them to betray the way God made them. In other words, it is asking the impossible and the undesirable.

It is impossible because God created us, male and female, with tremendous desire for sexual pleasure. Now he also, as we have repeated numerous times in this book, reserved the "one-flesh" bond of sexual intercourse for marriage. That is why lust is forbidden, because it is a drive that plots and manipulates for the purpose of merely physical consummation.

> To tell singles not to desire sex or to forbid the poetic anticipation of it before marriage is to ask them to betray the way God made them.

Desire, in contrast, is a God-given impulse that ultimately draws two people together. But what is a single man or woman to do with their desires in the typically long period between sexual maturity and marriage? Remember that this is an issue that is accentuated by the modern practice of delaying marriage till long after puberty.

The Bible does not address this question directly, so again we are in the realm of wisdom, not law. Nowhere does the Bible condemn the feelings of sexual desire. Indeed, and this will surprise some, nowhere does the Bible condemn or prohibit masturbation, though countless young people have been made to feel tremendous guilt at drawing pleasure and relief in this way.

What is the difference between masturbation that is full of lust and self-pleasuring that is full of goodness? The best way to enunciate the difference is to contrast a holy imagination with pornography. Pornography turns desire to lust as it makes one a voyeur of another's sexual activity. All pornography is centered on the power one has to compel another to do as you demand; therefore, it is about control, dominance, and ultimately degradation. All masturbation that finds its core image centered on power, use, and degradation violates true self-pleasure. It makes the heart small and cheap.

On the other hand, masturbation that imagines the man or woman who by character, generosity, and love—let alone beauty and desire—arouses you is meant to stir the body and heart to pleasure. The warning is to not let the flame consume the boundaries of honor and care before one is ready—both personally and relationally. In other words, the woman instructs the daughters (and us, particularly single people like the daughters) not to indulge the passion of the present until there is a future for a relationship.

But once the time is right, the love and its physical intimacies are glorious, as the poet indicates in what might be the most striking and powerful poems in the collection. The daughters of Jerusalem open with a question that is similar to the one that the woman asked in 3:6, perhaps connecting the present poem with the earlier poem on the grandeur of love as reflected in the opulence of Solomon's wedding.

> Who is this that comes up from the wilderness,
> leaning on her lover? (8:5a)

The wilderness, in contrast to the city, is the place of love, and now the woman returns from the place of intimacy. But rather than answering the daughters' question, she addresses the man in a memory of their lovemaking.

> Under the apple tree, I aroused you.
> There your mother conceived you.
> There the one who gave you birth conceived you. (8:5b)

In our earlier analysis of the poem in 2:1–7, we noted the erotic overtones of the setting under the apple tree. The apple, like all trees, provides shade and cover, a sense of privacy, but it is also a symbol of fertility, an appropriate place for intimacy.

As the second and third lines of the poetic triplet indicate, there is an indirect allusion, a hint of childbirth in the woman's comment. They made love at the place where the man's mother made love to his father with the result of his birth.

The Song never speaks directly of children as a result of intercourse between the man and the woman but here speaks indirectly of it. The purpose of avoiding direct mention of children is to accentuate that sex is prized for the pleasure of it and how it draws a husband and a wife closer, not only physically, but also emotionally and spiritually. To put it another way, the purpose of sex is not only, or even primarily, for the production of children, but for the joy of it.

The Song is thus repeating the same message as Genesis 2:24 when it defines marriage as a process of leaving parents, joining two lives together, and becoming one flesh, the latter a clear allusion to sexual intercourse. Marriage is not further defined as having children.

Her love for the man leads the woman to make a bold request of him.

> Set me like a seal on your heart,
>> like a seal on your arm. (8:6a)

To understand her request, we need to know the function of seals in ancient Near Eastern and, in particular, Israelite society. A seal was a small object that was usually made out of stone and was engraved with a particular mark that when rolled across a soft surface, such as clay, would leave an impression. The particular mark was unique to the owner of the seal, and the resultant impression identified the person as the owner of the marked object. While the ancient Near East knows of cylinder seals that were rolled across the object to leave the mark, in Israel the typical seal was a stamp seal that, as the name suggests, was simply stamped on the object. It is the latter that we should probably hold in our mind as we picture the request of the woman.

> To put it another way, the purpose of sex is not only, or even primarily, for the production of children, but for the joy of it.

The woman by asking the man to set her like a seal on his heart and arm is thus asking the man to display her ownership of him in a public way. Indeed, by specifying the heart (inside) and his arm (outside), she wants him, body and soul, to completely acknowledge their loyal love for each other. It is one of the most striking images in the poetic ensemble. First, it is radical that a woman in that culture would ask a man to publicly bear her name as the owner of his life. Second, it implies the embedding of a mark or scar that serves as a brand of loyalty. He is hers, and he is loyal to no other. It trivializes the concept to consider this a form of tattoo, but in our culture of transitory impermanence a tattoo is not far from what she is asking.

In our twenty-first-century world, the idea of someone owning another person is disturbing. We want to insist on our independence; we fear our vulnerability by opening ourselves up to another person in this way.

Indeed, there are risks in such wholehearted commitment to another person. We open ourselves up to pain if the person to whom we so give ourselves tries to manipulate or use us, or refuses to reciprocate by offering himself or herself to us.

But to live without risk is to live a bland, lonely life. Risk, however, should only be taken if the evidence of the present indicates that the person to whom one offers himself or herself is a person who will not abuse the relationship.

The woman trusts that the man won't use the power she gives him for his own self-serving purposes, and it is safe to assume that the man would in return offer himself to her in a similar way. In the New Testament, Paul makes clear the mutuality of this giving of each other within the marriage when he says, "The wife does not have authority over her own body but yields it to her husband. In the same way, the husband does not have authority over his own body but yields it to his wife" (1 Cor. 7:4 NIV).

The woman goes on to announce why she is willing to take the risk. Such love is powerful; indeed, it is equal to the most powerful forces, forces that threaten extinction.

> For love is as strong as Death;
>> passion is as tenacious as the Grave.
> Its flame is an intense fire,
>> a god-like flame.
> Many waters are not able to extinguish love,
>> nor rivers flood it.
> Even if a person gave all the wealth of his house for love,
>> he would be completely despised. (8:6b–7)

Her desire for him is strong, as strong as Death. Death is an irresistible and inevitable force. Nothing can stop it, as the book of Ecclesiastes makes clear.

> Then I turned and observed something else under the sun. That is, the race is not to the swift, the battle not to the mighty, nor is food for the wise, nor

wealth to the clever, nor favor to the intelligent, but time and chance happen to all of them.

Indeed, no one knows his time. Like fish that are entangled in an evil net and like birds caught in a snare, so people are ensnared in an evil time, when it suddenly falls on them. (Eccles. 9:11–12)[3]

Furthermore, in the ancient Near East, Death is personified as a god of great power. In Canaanite mythology that god's name is Mot ("Death"), whose power is such that he at least temporarily defeats and swallows Ba'al, who represents fertility, the power of life. Here the woman boldly asserts that love, her love, is even stronger than Death. It is, in other words, irresistible, resolute, and unshakeable.

In the next line, she accentuates her thought by announcing that love is as tenacious as the Grave. We capitalize "Grave" because, like Death, it is here personified, seen as an active power that seeks to overwhelm a person. But love is its equal and will not be defeated by Death or the Grave.

Nor will it be overwhelmed by chaos. The waters in Scripture often stand for those forces that seek to overcome and efface the order of the creation (Pss. 18:16; 29:3; 69:1, etc.).

Love stands against all these forces of evil. After all, "its flame is an intense fire, a god-like flame." Evil and its debris cannot stand before the burning, holy fire of love. Sex is then not really the hottest part of the flame. As much as we think of sexual joy as hot and full of passion, it is the love in, for, through, with, against, between (and every preposition we can use) one's spouse that is the reversal of death, the grave, and chaos. It is a phenomenally bold statement: love—including sexual joy between loyal lovers—trumps death, the waters of chaotic evil, and the power of the grave.

> Love—including sexual joy between loyal lovers—trumps death, the waters of chaotic evil, and the power of the grave.

How can this be true? It is true when you see the widow who speaks of her deceased spouse in the present. He is there in memory and in the keen and sometimes excruciating anticipation of their reunion. Love remembers and therefore redeems the past; it anticipates and therefore redeems the future, thus creating a present that is not possible without love. Love truly wins; it truly reverses the horror and heartache of death.

Before going on, perhaps we should add a word about the "god-like flame," since translations differ here. On the one hand, some translations take the Hebrew as a "raging" (NRSV) or "fierce" (Revised English Bible) or "blazing" (New American Bible) or "mighty" (NIV) flame, while others indicate that it is a "flame of Yahweh" (New Jerusalem Bible). The difference in translations arises because of dispute over the appearance of *yah* at the end of the Hebrew word for flame. *Yah* is sometimes the shortened form of the divine name Yahweh, the name God revealed to Moses at the burning bush (Exod. 3). But it can also be used as a superlative suffix, which in this verse would turn the word "flame" into the most intense flame imaginable.

Our translation, "god-like flame," splits the difference. But it also preserves something important that the translation "flame of Yahweh" does not. The poet who wrote the songs that constitute the Song of Songs is very intentionally avoiding mentioning God. Here, as we have seen elsewhere (in the oath formula directed at the daughters), he hints at God's name (and presence), but he never makes it explicit.

But why? Why doesn't God play a bigger role in the Song?

It's not that God is uncomfortable with sex. Indeed, the Song, as part of the Bible, witnesses to the fact that God loves sex, as does his creation of male and female to enjoy a "one-flesh" union (see the conclusion).

The hinting at God's name shows that he is indeed present, but he makes his presence known indirectly in a way that preserves the privacy of the bedroom. Like parents who rejoice in their child's intimate relationship with his or her spouse without intruding on them, so God relishes the idea that the man and the woman enjoy their private intimacy with one another.

17

Tears of Laughter

Our group is over. The last night as we talked about what we each had gained through the group I cried enough to scare Lois. I walked out to Agnes after we had communion and prayed for each other, hoping the engine would fail so I could go back into Jon's house and spend the night. Agnes started up like a dream.

I wanted Lois to come by and have one last talk before I drove off, like she had done after one of the earlier gatherings. Her face is far less puffy now, and her skin doesn't elide into red every time she talks. She had makeup on, and she was not wearing her Buster Brown shoes. She sat with Amihan on the couch, and the two of them squawked in laughter as they did impressions of my spacey demeanor the first night. I have never felt more wonderfully mocked.

Each person shared some of what they gained through the group. It all feels like a blur, but I will never forget Lois's tears. She said, "I don't hate sex like I did. I may not be ready or ever ready to be married again, but I feel so happy not blaming sex for all that I have suffered." Then she looked at us and her voice dropped nearly to a whisper, "And maybe I am closer to saying sex is a good gift from God."

I spoke after Lois and told them I want to live and die for love. I don't want to spend the rest of my life flirting, conquering, being conquered, and then fleeing love. I want to love with all the passion, playfulness, honor, and goodness of this erotic Sex Song. It was that simple. My desires seem to be changing.

I am sad that my last girlfriend had to end our relationship with a text-message poem. I am sadder that I didn't have the courage to talk to her face-to-face and tell her thank you. I need to tell her face-to-face that I was not man enough, then, to believe that love wins and mocks death. I am brave enough to tell her today. I know what I know now. I also know she is not the woman I am meant to love and whose name I am meant to plant on my heart.

I know too that I am not the man any woman ought rightly to ask to bear her seal. Not today; likely not tomorrow either. I have thought back to the meal I had with Jon early on, when he asked if I considered any of the sexual trysts when I was young as sexual abuse. I shuddered and deferred his question. His question has been like a fish bone in my throat. It is not enough to kill me, but enough to keep me from being able to swallow easily.

I have a sexual history that I need time to ponder and need a context in which to talk about and grieve. I will find a good therapist who neither indulges sexuality as a so-called natural need nor is afraid to talk about my signs of decadence. I need to find someone who knows brokenness from the depths of their own desire and knows beauty as the promise of what love births.

I want to prepare my heart and body for love. I don't want it awakened before its time, but I want my dreams prior to waking up to be full of sensuous anticipation, holy arousal, and of the coming of the woman who will mark me with the promise of that god-like fire.

May it be.

Even more so I need to let the god-like fire of the Holy Trinity mature my body and heart. I am new to all this God thought, but what I know now in a way that I didn't before is that God created sex for our pleasure with one another, but no less for our pleasure with him. A friend of mine who knows I am swerving toward God gave me a book of John Donne's poems. Who knew? The man is wild in the ways of sensuality and the divine. My friend told me to read "Holy Sonnet 14."

Batter my heart, three-person'd God, for you
As yet but knock, breathe, shine, and seek to mend;
That I may rise, and stand, o'erthrow me, and bend
Your force, to break, blow, burn, and make me new.
I, like an usurp'd town, to another due,
Labour to admit you, but O, to no end.
Reason, your viceroy in me, me should defend,
But is captived, and proves weak or untrue.
Yet dearly I love you, and would be loved fain,
But am betroth'd unto your enemy;
Divorce me, untie, or break that knot again,
Take me to you, imprison me, for I,
Except you enthrall me, never shall be free,
Nor ever chaste, except you ravish me.[1]

Just as I had no idea where this study would take me, so I don't know what is ahead, other than knowing, with Donne, that I will never "be free, Nor ever chaste, except you ravish me."

May it be.

Conclusion

After the Glory

As we have observed from the start, the Song of Songs is not a narrative with a plot that has a beginning, middle, and end. It does not tell a single story. The Song is a collection of love poems, though these love poems serve a common purpose and thus have an organic and coherent feel to them. The common purpose is first to celebrate physical intimacy, but there is also the warning that love is risky and not easily experienced.

The celebration of sex in the Song fits into the broader biblical picture of sexuality that begins in the Garden of Eden. Genesis 2 ends with the statement that "Adam and his wife were both naked, and they felt no shame" (v. 25 NIV). When God first created humanity, there were no barriers to a harmonious and pleasurable relationship—sexually, emotionally, psychologically, and spiritually. Because they had a harmonious relationship with God, they had a harmonious relationship with each other.

They were in the Garden naked and enjoying each other. We can presume this meant not only enjoying one another's bodies sexually, but also enjoying the companionship of intimately exploring creation together. We have no clue if they played tennis or backgammon, but both games are a result of the creative urge to explore our physical abilities and the complexity of what we often refer to as chance. Adam and Eve explored creation, including one another's bodies, to better know the heart of their Creator. They lived in creation and explored it to discover what it means to be human and what it means to be in relationship with God as human beings. It is this context that is important to explore as we consider how sex reveals the heart of God.

Notice the difference between seeing the Song as an allegory and seeing it as an anthology of erotic love poems. An allegory forces the poetry into a story that often tells immensely important stories about God. Yet, even when the material written in the Song is wise in and of itself as a reflection on the heart of God, an allegorical reading contorts this wisdom by forcing the Bible into a form it can't bear.

When we take the other approach—namely, by reading the Song as a collection of love poems—we would be foolish to think that we don't learn vastly important things about the heart of God through considering a passionate, loyal, flourishing love relationship. In fact, what we learn about God is immensely important, but it is learned indirectly, poetically rather than through the "heavier hand" of prose. These poems help us understand God's love of pleasure and play, his commitment to remain faithful to us even when we are adulterous, and finally that he loves to see human beings flourish and grow in fruitfulness and joy.

> These poems help us understand God's love of pleasure and play, his commitment to remain faithful to us even when we are adulterous, and finally that he loves to see human beings flourish and grow in fruitfulness and joy.

Pleasure and Play

The God of creation likes to play. Not only is he creative, but he also loves to recreate. Say the word "re-create" as if you are talking about redemption. Now say the word as if you are talking about play. Different spelling and enunciation, but etymologically it derives from the same core concept. God loves to restore creation so that play without shame, cruelty, and violence can continue. The Garden was a big play day that God entered into during the cool of the day so that he could hang out with Adam and Eve and join them in the pleasure of their discovery.

There was no shame. There were no parental issues with God. There was no sexual fear, perversion, or disgust. There was only pleasure, play, and joy. God would not have intruded into their sexuality as if he were a voyeur, but there would have been sexual discussions, conversation, and learning that would simply have been playful.

It is God who loves sex, whereas his enemy, the evil one, hates it. The pleasure of a good orgasm and the arousal of playful flirtation tell us not only that God loves sex but also that he loves the joy that comes from being part of the giving and receiving of pleasure.

> It is God who loves sex, whereas his enemy, the evil one, hates it.

To consider God as a lover of pleasure demands we turn away from ideas of God being negative toward our sexuality. Even when there is failure and brokenness, his heart toward us is grieved, not abandoning, furious, or disgusted. God's love of pleasure is utterly in alignment with his faithfulness.

Fidelity and Commitment

God is our faithful, committed spouse, whereas we are far more often like the lover described in Ezekiel 16, whose beauty, given by God, is used to hook up with idols that are not God. Song of Songs is a realistic book. While proclaiming the redemption of sex, it acknowledges that it is an already-but-not-yet redemption. In other words, though God-blessed sexual pleasure is possible, it comes in glimpses. The struggle is still present, as we have seen in the poems discussed in the chapters on sexual struggles (chaps. 12 and 13) and in the warning to the daughters of Jerusalem not to "arouse or awaken love until it so desires" (see chap. 16, "The Glory of Sex").

Accordingly, it would betray the message of the Song of Songs, as well as present human experience, if the Song ended with a poem that reflected final and lasting contentment and satisfaction. Not surprisingly, since the Song is not simply an idealistic romantic reverie, the final poem acknowledges that, this side of heaven, at least, while orgasm brings a type of closure to sought-after sexual desire, it is not the end of the story.

Desire soon arises again. Thus, the Song closes with an interchange between the man and the woman.

THE MAN
You who dwell in the gardens,
    companions are listening,
    let me hear your voice!

THE WOMAN
Sneak away, my lover, and be like a gazelle,
    or a young stag on the mountains of spice. (8:13–14)

Thus, the Song ends with the man and the woman apart from each other, yearning for union again in the garden of love. Satisfaction is not final; love never fully satisfies as we desire. We desire more than any one relationship can provide, and yet to seek from others what one can't fully satisfy is to create even more emptiness and sorrow. We are both blessed and cursed by desire. And we are never perfectly faithful to God, our lover, or to ourselves as we wrestle with desire. Only God is faithful in his desire for us.

The Song of Songs invites us to intensify our desire for sex and play. The by-product is to increase our desire for an Edenic sexuality that will only be fully possible in the new heavens and earth. This of course brings up the question of whether there will be sex in heaven.

Even to ask the question makes people squirm. To some, sex is so tainted that it couldn't possibly be part of our heavenly experience. Though it is true that sex, like all of human nature and experience, has been deeply disrupted by sin, we should never forget that it is God who made us sexual creatures and that sexual pleasure is his good gift to us.

To others, sex is a physical, bodily act. Won't we be spiritual beings, like the angels, in heaven?

For this latter view, one might even turn to Jesus's response to the Sadducees in Luke 20:27–40 for support. The Sadducees do not believe in the afterlife, so they make fun of Jesus's view on the matter by drawing his attention to a woman who had been married multiple times. They then intend to ridicule Jesus when they ask him, "Now then, at the resurrection whose wife will she be, since the seven were married to her?" (v. 33 NIV).

Jesus responds by contrasting the present age with the future age by saying, "those who are considered worthy of taking part in the age to come and in the resurrection from the dead will neither marry nor be given in marriage, and they can no longer die; for they are like the angels" (20:35–36a NIV).

That seems to settle it. We will be like the angels. There will be no marriage and certainly no sex.

But what are angels? They are spiritual beings to be sure, but we go too far when we say that as such they are incapable of something like sexual acts. What Jesus is saying is that they do not marry and there won't be marriage in heaven, but he says nothing about sex or something like sex in heaven.

Indeed, in the writings of Jews from the time of Jesus and the century before (such as *1 Enoch* and *Jubilees*), it is very clear that Jews at that time thought that angels were at least capable of sexual acts since they interpreted the enigmatic story of the "sons of God" marrying the "daughters of humans" in Genesis 6:1–4 (NIV) as angels impregnating human women.

And in any case, Jesus does not intend to say that we are like the angels in every way. Indeed, the New Testament consistently teaches that in heaven we will not live a purely spiritual existence, but we will have bodies—resurrection bodies.

And why would we think that a divine gift as enjoyable and pleasurable as sex would be lacking in heaven? But it is not only enjoyable; it is an experience in which a person can lose oneself in the other person. In other words, two people become "one flesh." Though described physically, this oneness is felt not just in the body but also in the soul.

Again, the Bible does not give us a detailed description of what heaven will be like, and so we must be careful in our assertions. Much is shrouded in mystery, but we know that whatever its precise shape, it will be wonderful.

We will, after all, once again have a harmonious relationship with God, as in the Garden of Eden. Indeed, we will have an even better relationship with God in heaven than Adam and Eve did in the Garden. This truth is taught by the picture of the New Jerusalem having two trees of life rather than a single one (Rev. 22:1–5).

If our relationship with God will surpass the harmony of the Garden, then perhaps it is not a stretch to expect that our relationships with one another as humans will be deeper, better, more pleasurable than the relationship between Adam and Eve in the Garden. Indeed, perhaps that is what sex gives us just a glimpse of—namely, the deeper relationship, body and soul, that we will share as God's people and will enjoy for eternity in his presence.

It is God's faithful, pursuing, passionate love that secures for us this promise, not our faithfulness. Even when we are faithful, it is his faithfulness that first called us into this promise, and when we are not, it is his commitment to us that secures what we cannot satisfy. As much as sexuality is a mutual interplay of delight and pleasure, it is only secured by his love.

Flourishing and Fruitfulness

Sex in the Garden is not primarily about procreation. Procreation is hinted at and is eclipsed by the sensuous delight of pursuit and pleasure. Sex is about human flourishing that fills both hearts with a fullness of being. Sometimes sex results in a womb filled with the rich gift of a child, but that fecundity is not the apex or the goal of sex; it is the penultimate purpose. First and foremost, sex is our connective link to what it means to worship. Worship is the interplay of awe and gratitude. We are amazed at the goodness of God—amazement is wonder with awe.

Our lover is meant to take our breath away. And our lover's body is meant to give us a taste of holy wonder that, at unexpected and often unexplained moments, makes us shudder with the awe of being in the presence of someone utterly different, other. Yet true worship also involves being grateful for a gift we could not create on our own or deserve as if we earned it. Gratitude acknowledges we are bound to and need the other. We are the undeserved recipients of a freely given grace.

Sex is meant to bring a holy "wow" and "yes" to the interplay of our mutual pleasure. The prompting of worship—awe and gratitude—is unbecoming and untenable to put on the shoulders of a mere human being. My spouse can prompt worship, but she is never meant to be the object of my deepest adoration. Only God. Only the one who made me to know the fruit of flourishing worship is to receive my deepest "wow" and "yes." And when the face and body of God is revealed through my lover Jesus, then I am given the wonder and awe of being called friend, not an enemy or a slave.

Human flourishing occurs at its richest in freedom from accusation. We flourish when we are fully known and not bound to fear, resentment, or shame. We give birth to newness and possibility only to the degree we bless desire, celebrate beauty, risk nakedness, and join God in the utter delight of his pleasure.

And this is his intent for our sexuality. Glory to the One who made us holy, whole, and sexual.

Notes

Chapter 1: Song of Songs: A Holy and Erotic Book

1. Tremper Longman, *Song of Songs*, New International Commentary on the Old Testament (Grand Rapids: Eerdmans, 2001).

2. *B. Sanhedrin* 101a, quoted in R. E. Murphy, *The Song of Songs*, Hermeneia (Minneapolis: Fortress, 1990), 13.

3. *M. Yadayim* 3.5, quoted in Murphy, *Song of Songs*, 6.

4. For a translation of the Targum, see Y. Sabart, *An Old Neo-Aramaic Version of the Targum on the Song of Songs* (Wiesbaden: Harrassowitz, 1991).

5. For examples of ancient Egyptian love poetry, see Longman, *Song of Songs*, 49–54.

6. The analogy is drawn by M. Pope, *Song of Songs* (Garden City, NY: Doubleday, 1977), 115.

7. Jerome, Letter cvii, in vol. 6 of *The Nicene and Post-Nicene Fathers*, 2nd ser., ed. Philip Schaff and Henry Wace (Peabody, MA: Hendrickson, 1994), 194, quoted in Pope, *Song of Songs*, 119.

8. John Wesley, *Explanatory Notes upon the Old Testament* (Bristol, England: Gale ECCO, 1965), quoted in R. M. Davidson, "Theology of Sexuality in the Song of Songs: Return to Eden," *Andrews University Seminary Studies* 27 (1989): 1–19.

9. Reading the Song through the biblical lens of God as husband has a surface similarity to an allegorical approach but is distinguished from it in two significant ways. First, the allegorical approach bypasses the reading of the book as a love poem describing the relationship between a man and a woman. Our theological reading takes the book as such a love poem and then says that the marriage relationship throws light on our relationship with God because of the pervasive use of the marriage metaphor throughout the Bible. Second, unlike the allegorical approach, our interpretation does not press the details as having symbolic value (for example, the breasts of 1:13 as the Old and New Testaments).

Chapter 4: The Dance of Desire

1. M. L. Chivers, M. C. Seto, M. L. Lalumiere, E. Laan, and T. Girmbos, "Agreement of Self-Reported and Genital Measures of Sexual Arousal in Men and Women: A Meta-Analysis," *Archives of Sexual Behavior* 39 (2010): 5–56.

2. P. C. Regan and E. Berscheid, "Beliefs about the State, Goals, and Objects of Sexual Desire," *Journal of Sex and Marital Therapy* 22 (1996): 110–20.

3. M. Meana, "Elucidating Women's (Hetero)sexual Desire: Definitional Challenges and Content Expansion," *Journal of Sex Research* 47 (2010): 104–22; K. McCall and C. Meston, "Cues Resulting in Sexual Activity in Women," *Journal of Sexual Medicine* 3 (2006): 838–52.

4. F. Toates, "An Integrative Theoretical Framework for Understanding Sexual Motivation, Arousal, and Behavior," *Journal of Sex Research* 46 (2009): 168–93.

5. J. Hiller, "Gender Differences in Sexual Motivation," *Journal of Men's Health and Gender* 2 (2005): 339–45.

6. B. J. Ellis and D. Symons, "Sex Differences in Sexual Fantasy: An Evolutionary Psychological Approach," *Journal of Sex Research* 27 (1990): 527–55.

7. Ibid.

8. For more information regarding the neurochemical and neuroanatomical systems involved in sexual excitation and inhibition, see J. G. Pfaus, "Pathways of Sexual Desire," *Journal of Sexual Medicine* 6 (2009): 1506–33.

9. D. J. Kavanagh, J. Andrade, and J. May, "Imaginary Relish and Exquisite Torture: The Elaborated Intrusion Theory of Desire," *Psychological Review* 112 (2005): 446–67.

10. A degree of anxiety can indeed increase attraction and desire, as seen by an experiment where men on a high suspension bridge were more likely to express interest to a female interviewer than men on more stable bridges. See D. G. Dutton and A. P. Aron, "Some Evidence for Heightened Sexual Attraction under Conditions of High Anxiety," *Journal of Personality and Social Psychology* 30 (1974): 510–17.

11. "This is a poem, not a travel itinerary," so C. Exum, *Song of Songs: A Commentary*, Old Testament Library (Louisville: Westminster John Knox, 2005), 169.

12. G. Hagman, "The Sense of Beauty," *International Journal of Psycho-Analysis* 83 (2002): 661–74.

13. R. Briggs, *SA.ZI.GA: Ancient Mesopotamian Potency Incantations* (Locust Valley, NY: Augustin, 1967).

Chapter 7: The Intrigue of Beauty

1. H. H. Sachs, "Beauty, Life and Death," *American Imago* 1 (1940): 81–133.

2. L. Ryken, J. Wilhoit, and T. Longman III, eds., *Dictionary of Biblical Imagery* (Downers Grove, IL: InterVarsity, 1998), 217.

3. The attractiveness of red lips spans culture and time, as research has shown that women wearing red lipstick are approached more quickly and more often than other women. See N. Gueguen, "Does Red Lipstick Really Attract Men? An Evaluation in a Bar," *International Journal of Psychological Studies* 4 (2012): 206–9.

4. O. Keel, *The Song of Songs*, Continental Commentary (Minneapolis: Fortress Press, 1994), 147.

5. The release of certain neurochemicals in orgasm can replicate the same feeling of a heroin addict being high from opiates. See J. R. Georgiadis, "Exposing Orgasm in the Brain: A Critical Eye," *Sexual Relationship Therapy* (2011): 342–55. Desire for cocaine in cocaine-dependent men rose when either viewing erotic stimuli or being exposed to a cocaine-related cue. See L. O. Bauer and H. R. Kranzler, "Electroencephalographic Activity and Mood in Cocaine-Dependent Outpatients: Effects of Cocaine Cue Exposure," *Biological Psychiatry* 36 (1994): 189–97.

Chapter 10: The Fantasy of Sexual Play

1. Attractiveness of a face has been seen to be judged by how close it is to the central tendency to the mean of the population, a face that is a composite average or prototype.

See I. H. Langlois and I. A. Roggman, "Attractive Faces Are Only Average," *Psychological Science* 1 (1990): 115–21.

2. D. T. Sanchez, A. K. Kiefer, and O. Ybarra, "Sexual Submissiveness in Women: Costs for Sexual Autonomy and Arousal," *Personality and Social Psychology Bulletin* 32 (2006): 512–24.

Chapter 12: The Struggle toward Intimacy, Part 1

1. A. J. Bridges, R. Wosnitzer, E. Scharrer, C. Sun, and R. Liberman, "Aggression and Sexual Behavior in Best-selling Pornography Videos: A Content Analysis Update," *Violence against Women* 16 (2010): 1065–85.

Chapter 13: The Struggle toward Intimacy, Part 2

1. N. D. Kristof and S. WuDunn, *Half the Sky: Turning Oppression into Opportunity for Women Worldwide* (2008; repr., New York: Vintage, 2010).

2. T. Longman III, *How to Read Proverbs* (Downers Grove, IL: InterVarsity, 2002), 28–36.

Chapter 16: The Glory of Sex

1. M. H. Pope, *Song of Songs* (Garden City, NY: Doubleday, 1977), 435.

2. See the excellent treatment of Jesus's words in D. Willard, *The Divine Conspiracy* (San Francisco: Harper, 1998), 177–93.

3. Translation and commentary may be found in T. Longman III, *Ecclesiastes*, New International Commentary on the Old Testament (Grand Rapids: Eerdmans, 1998), 232–33.

Chapter 17: Tears of Laughter

1. John Donne, "Holy Sonnet 14," in *The Complete English Poems*, Penguin Classics (New York: Penguin, 1971), 314–15.

Dan Allender (MDiv, Westminster Theological Seminary; MS, Barry College; PhD, Michigan State University) is professor of counseling psychology and is former president of the Seattle School of Theology and Psychology in Seattle, Washington. He travels and speaks extensively on sexual-abuse recovery, love and forgiveness, worship, and other related topics. Allender is the author of fourteen books, including *The Wounded Heart*, which has sold over four hundred thousand copies. He is married to Becky, and they live on Bainbridge Island in Washington. They have two daughters and one son, and two grandsons and one granddaughter. For the survival of his body and soul, Dan likes to fly-fish.

Tremper Longman III (PhD, Yale University) is the Robert H. Gundry Professor of Biblical Studies at Westmont College in Santa Barbara, California. He has authored, coauthored, or edited numerous books, including *An Introduction to the Old Testament*, *How to Read Proverbs*, *The Baker Illustrated Bible Dictionary*, and commentaries on Job, Proverbs, Ecclesiastes, Song of Songs, Jeremiah and Lamentations, and Daniel. Tremper is married to Alice, and they live in Santa Barbara, California. They have three sons and two granddaughters. For fun and exercise, Tremper plays squash.

GOD LOVES SEX

the companion video series

The authors of *God Loves Sex* are stunned when they meet Malcolm, the character they created, now off the page and in the flesh.

Malcolm has come looking for answers. After completing his group study on the Song of Songs, he has met a woman named Elizabeth and finds himself drawn to her. His desires raise further questions and concerns about sexuality, marriage, and God.

Through a series of provocative conversations, the three men delve into the book's themes of sexual desire and holiness as they engage Malcolm's struggles, hopes, and fears around erotic love and faithfulness.

This video series is available at

theallendercenter.org

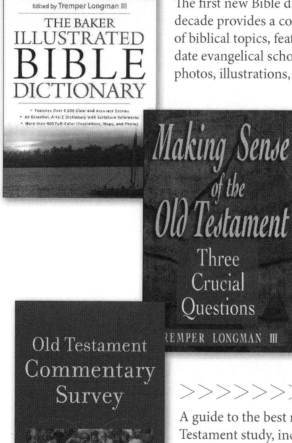

Tremper Longman III

"[Longman] sets the record straight, arguing that the book of Proverbs is indeed a book about theology as well as prudential wisdom."

—R. Albert Mohler Jr., *Preaching*

"A work of inestimable pastoral and practical value."

—**Eugene H. Merrill,** distinguished professor of Old Testament studies, Dallas Theological Seminary

BakerBooks

BakerBooks.com
Available wherever books and ebooks are sold.

The Allender Center
at The Seattle School

Made in the USA
Coppell, TX
01 July 2020